David Thomisse

Sound and vision
on your Web site

First published in the United Kingdom in 2001 by Hachette UK
ISBN 1 84202 084 6

Designed by M2M / Typeset in Sabon MT / Printed and bound in Germany

English translation by Prose Unlimited

Concept and editorial direction: Ghéorghiï Vladimirovitch Grigorieff

Additional editorial assistance: Simon Woolf, Derek Atkins, Rodney Cuff

A CIP catalogue for this book is available from the British Library.

Trademarks/Registered Trademarks

Hachette UK
Cassell & Co
The Orion Publishing Group
Wellington House
125 Strand
London
WC2R 0BB

Table of Contents

INTRODUCTION

An animated, dynamic Web site is attractive and user friendly. Net surfers feel they're visiting an active site. With a little imagination, they can forget that they're looking at the screen of a machine, and instead feel they're dealing with a living, talking being. Such a site features *multimedia* information for the eye (animation), the ear (sounds) and the sense of touch (keyboard and mouse). The effectiveness of such a combination of sensory input can be gauged from the success of educational CD-ROMs and video games.

A 'dynamic' Web site is one with both dynamic content and dynamic presentation. But these two conceptually distinct aspects are not mutually exclusive; they're interrelated and interconnected, or *interactive* as the jargon has it.

In this book, we'll look at the technologies that enable you to create a dynamic, interactive and user-friendly Web site.

Dynamic information

Not long ago, Web pages were static, conveying information to an otherwise passive visitor. But things have moved a long way in recent years. Various technologies, grouped under the term *scripting server languages,* have breathed life into information. Thanks to *database processing*, *forms* and *cookies*, the contents of a site can now be updated on a regular basis, information can be customised to suit the visitor, and pages can be changed as the user proceeds. Today, surfers have become active – or should we say interactive? Indeed, on certain sites they can make their own contribution – for example, publish an article or send photos to put on the site.

We don't deal with the dynamic processing of data in this book, although the scripting languages we will be dealing with can play an important role on this front too.

The interactive Web

The principle of *hypertext*, the linchpin of the Internet, laid the foundations of an interactive approach to information. Information came alive thanks to links that enabled a user to jump straight to the heart of a document or from document to document. But this approach, although revolutionary when applied to the Internet, paled by comparison with other multimedia technologies such as interactive CD-ROMs.

The interactive and dynamic functions of Web pages were boosted considerably with the emergence of scripting languages, which are dealt with in the first part of this book.

The animated, multimedia Web

In the second part, we'll take stock of the current state of animation on the Net. At first it consisted of a few voluminous (albeit highly compressed) images that were slow to display. Gradually, however, as data transfer rates increased with faster modems, and as compression technologies became more sophisticated, the Web got on the move. Yet these developments, although groundbreaking at times, have not turned Web pages into cinema screens. Persistent barriers (chiefly to do with compatibility problems and the size of files) still hinder the display of video and animated images on Web sites.

The purpose of this book

Such a vast subject is not easy to treat and cannot possibly be covered fully within a small book. So we won't try to turn you into an expert with a full grasp of all the intricacies of the dynamic and interactive technologies of the Internet. Instead, we'll help you to understand the basics through an overview of these technologies and a practical introduction to them. The best school for more advanced study is probably the Web itself, but the jargon of the dynamic Web can seem an impenetrable jungle for the newcomer. This book will prepare you to find your way through this jungle and to pick and choose what you like and enjoy.

PREREQUISITES

Prior knowledge

This book is intended for those already familiar with *HTML* (see in particular the book devoted to this language in the current series). We're dealing with complementary technologies – each of the languages that we cover (JavaScript, DHTML, etc.) is related to HTML and works alongside it. So we're constantly referring back to HTML, and will assume that brief references are sufficient for you to know what we're talking about. When we do focus on particular HTML tags, they will often be for advanced functions and will require you to be familiar with the basics of the language.

Hardware and software requirements

Things are moving extremely fast in information technology. Such unrelenting progress means that users must constantly upgrade their hardware and software to capitalise fully on the latest advancements. This rather restrictive requirement weighs heavily on the Web, and 'up-to-the-minute' surfers must toe the line accordingly.

On the software front, all eyes are on the *browser*. Browser incompatibility, both vertical (between different versions of the same browser) and horizontal (between different browsers) limit a Webmaster's field of action. To minimise such differences, this book is geared to users of the latest readily available versions of the most widely used browsers on the market – at the time of writing, Internet Explorer 5.5 and Netscape 4.7.

The recent release of Netscape 6 is combined with a new version of JavaScript (1.5). The resulting change in syntax does not allow us to guarantee the full compatibility of all the examples provided in this book.

It is also a good idea to download at least some of the most recent and popular *plug-ins* for reading multimedia files (such as Flash, QuickTime and RealPlayer).

Finally, a simple text editor like Notepad will do just fine for writing code such as HTML or JavaScript. There are also many specialised script editors, offering debugging functions, use of colours, lists of function names and so forth. But such software, which can be expensive and more difficult to use, is not essential.

Note

How to test the examples given in the book:

1. Open Notepad and create a blank file.
2. Type the code in, exactly as displayed in the book (including the same spacing and type of brackets).
3. Save the file with the extension .htm (or .html).
4. Double-click the newly saved file, to open and view in your default browser.

PART I

The interactive Web and scripting languages

1. JavaScript

If you're familiar with the Internet, then you'll have come across the term *JavaScript*. Whether you've been aware of it or not, your favourite browser has already run dozens, indeed hundreds of JavaScript programs (also known as JavaScripts or just scripts) when you've been surfing.

These small scripts are responsible for a myriad of applications deployed when you download a Web page or carry out a specific action such as entering a password, displaying the time, viewing a drop-down menu, scrolling text or receiving error messages. But what exactly are they and what do they offer a Webmaster in search of interactivity?

JavaScript was developed by Netscape to boost the functionality of HTML. Based largely on the syntaxes of C/C++ and *Java*, this language is used to write scripts. A JavaScript is a script within an HTML document and is an integral part of the page code. When a browser downloads a Web page, it 'reads' and simultaneously *interprets* the code to run it. That's why we speak about languages that are *interpreted*, unlike *compiled* languages that have been previously translated into directly executable codes.

Java and JavaScript

Java, a language developed by Sun, must not be confused with JavaScript, although it can also (but not exclusively) be used to create applications for the Web. These are called Java *applets*, and we shall return to them in Chapter 4.

1.1. JavaScript syntax

This section is intended to provide a summary of the JavaScript syntax, and not to turn you into an expert JavaScript programmer. A more extensive treatment would require a book in itself, one far more voluminous than the present work.

More information on the JavaScript syntax is readily available on the sites referenced in Appendix C.

JavaScript objects and their properties

The *object* is a key notion of JavaScript. Objects combine assortments of disparate data, which may either be predefined or *native* objects, or else objects created by a JavaScript programmer. A native object can consist of a character string, a button, a link or an image, for example, or may comprise an entire HTML page, the browser or the display screen.

Like an HTML tag, which has *attributes* (e.g. the tag **<img>** with the attributes **align**, **border**, **height**, etc.), each of these objects has a certain number of properties (known as *variables*) which describe it or its constituent elements. The objects can be manipulated by programming and modifying these properties.

Example 1

The **document** object, which represents an entire HTML page, has numerous properties such as its background colour (**bgColor**), the title of the page (**title**) and also the various images (**Images**[]) or anchors (**anchors**[]) contained in the page.

The background colour of a document can thus be designated as follows:

document.bgColor

Syntax note 1

An object or one of its properties is accessed by its *qualified name* from the hierarchy of JavaScript objects presented in Appendix B. Each object is separated from its parent by a dot (.). In our example, in which **bgColor** is a property of the **document** object, the latter is at the top of the hierarchy of JavaScript objects. The list of qualifiers can be quite extensive, as in a case such as:

```
document.forms[0].elements[2].value =
"Click here"
```

This designates the value (the character string that will be displayed on the screen) of the third element (a button) of the first form on the page. Note that the numbering system that indicates an object in a page starts with 0. Thus, the first image of a document will be indicated by [0] and not by [1]. An object can be designated by its order of appearance in the document (between square brackets) or by its name. So if we've already named the form **my_form** and its third element **button3**, we can also access the button as follows:

document.my_form.button3.value = "Click here"

One more qualifying method can be used:

document.forms["my_form"].elements["button3"].value = "Click here"

To attribute a value to the background colour, we write:

document.bgColor = "#0000FF"

The **document** object designates the entire page, and the hexadecimal value **#0000FF** the colour blue. So the property 'background colour' of the object 'document' takes the value 'blue'. Note that the colours can also be designated directly by name rather than by hexadecimal value.

Syntax note 2

It is good practice to place a value, whether alphabetic or numeric, between quotation marks. Otherwise, in certain circumstances it will be considered as the name of an object or a variable, the value of which the interpreter will seek (in vain) elsewhere in the document. We adopt this convention in most instances throughout this book.

Functions and methods

You can apply certain actions to JavaScript objects. These are divided into *functions* and *methods*. Functions are generic, i.e. they can be applied to any object; methods are specific to a particular object. Just like objects and their properties, functions and methods can be native (to the JavaScript environment) or defined by the user.

Example 2

The function **write()**, which is attached to the object **document,** writes on the Web page the text entered between parentheses. For instance, **document.write("my phrase")** will display the character string "my phrase" on your browser screen. This character string is the *argument* of the function **write()**.

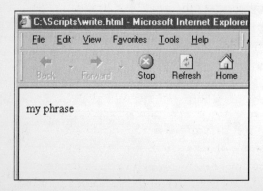

The arguments of a function are the values required to run that function. If you don't supply a character string for the function in Example 2, nothing will be displayed on the screen. In some cases, if a required argument is missing, the function will 'crash'.

The number of arguments depends on the function (its execution may require no argument at all or a sizeable number of arguments). Arguments are entered between parentheses and separated by a comma.

Function declaration

Using only the native JavaScript functions may often prove too restrictive. So you can create your own functions, as if you're inventing a recipe, the ingredients of which are drawn from the established grammar of JavaScript (objects, methods, etc.). As a general rule, you declare a function when its code need not be executed in the normal top-to-bottom sequence of the written program, but needs instead to be called at will from elsewhere, perhaps several times. It is then associated with a *condition* or an *event*. (We will come back later to events and conditional executions.) A function that you define can itself involve several native functions. Finally, a declared function must then be invoked in order to be executed.

Example 3

Let us imagine a simple personalised welcome message. The user can write his or her name (X) in an entry field on the form. Once confirmed, the following message will appear on the screen: "Hello, X!"

You can write the code for this small application as follows:

```
<FORM>
<INPUT TYPE="text" VALUE="">
<INPUT TYPE="button" VALUE="OK"
```

```
onClick="go(document.forms[0].elements[0].value)">
</FORM>

<SCRIPT LANGUAGE="JavaScript">
function go(name)
{ alert("Hello "+name+"!")
}
</SCRIPT>
```

The execution of this function entails waiting for an *event*: when you click **OK** on the form, an alert message is displayed. We first created the form, composed of an entry field and an OK-button. When the event **onClick** takes place (i.e. when we click on the button), the function **go()** is launched. The argument it contains is the value (of **name**) entered in the text field, which is accessed via its naming hierarchy.

The function itself is declared with the keyword **function**. Then comes the name of the function (which you can choose), followed by its single argument between parentheses. The name given to the argument is again up to you; the user will never see it, but it will acquire a value when the function is invoked using the string entered in the form's text field. The instructions (more usually known as *statements*) of the function are then placed between braces {}. In our example, we use the method **alert()**, which opens a window containing the message "Hello, " followed by the name entered by the user, and an exclamation mark.

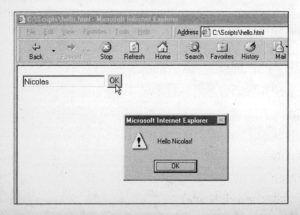

Variables

The arguments of a function can also be defined as variables. So we can program functions whose result will depend on the value of its arguments. Mathematical functions are a good illustration, but variables can also be highly interactive, especially in conjunction with forms. We have just seen an example of this.

A variable can take an alphabetic, a numeric or an inde-finite value.

Let's return to Example 2, and declare the character string to be displayed on the screen as a variable.

A variable is declared using the keyword **var**.

Example 4

```
var phrase;
phrase="my phrase";
document.write(phrase);
```

Once the variable **phrase** has been declared, an alphabetic value is assigned to it. So we get the same kind of result as in Example 2: the string "my phrase" is displayed on the screen, but with the added advantage that we have defined a variable whose value can be modified, e.g. when text is typed into a form.

Syntax note

When we declare an object, a variable or a function, we can use any character string except a series of JavaScript *reserved words*. These are listed in Appendix A. Note also that a semicolon separates one statement from the next.

Operators

As their name indicates, operators are used to carry out a series of operations, such as arithmetic (multiplica-

tion, subtraction, etc.), concatenation (assembling several character or variable strings) or comparison (equal,
less than, greater than …).

These operators offer countless possibilities. We will give
two examples here, admittedly simplistic but which nonetheless illustrate what operators are and what they do.

Example 5

Let's consider a simple multiplication:

document.write("3 times 4 = ", 3*4);

The result will be displayed on the screen as: "3 times 4
= 12".

The function has two arguments. The first is a character
string that will be displayed unchanged, because it is between quotation marks. The second consists of an arithmetic operation that uses the multiplication operator
(*); here, only the result of the JavaScript operation will
be displayed.

Here's a concatenation operation based on Example 4:

```
var phrase="my phrase";
document.write("I write " + phrase);
```

These two lines of code will display "I write my phrase" on the screen. Whereas the first component of the output string is explicitly given, the rest of it will vary, depending on the value of the variable **phrase**. We've already had a concatenation operation in Example 3, although we didn't mention it.

Syntax note

The name of a variable must not be placed between quotation marks – that would simply be a reference to a character string with the same letters as make up the name of the variable!

Control statements

Thanks to JavaScript control statements, an application can be run non-linearly. Without these statements, the browser would run the script from beginning to end, one time only, before continuing to interpret the code of the page.

There are two types of control statements:

▸ Conditional statements: **if (...) ... else** and **switch** apply a conditional test such as 'if' the specified condition is met, then the first operation will be carried out; 'else' the second operation will take place. **If...else** uses a binary test, whereas the **switch** statement allows a check against several values.

▸ Loop statements: **for, while, do ... while** and **break** can be used to repeat a statement or a set of statements several times or to stop them when a particular condition is met.

Events

Together with the control statements, events are the most interesting aspect of JavaScript for our purposes. They allow an action to be carried out at a given moment. The action is implemented by statements such as we have previously outlined, while the event defines the 'moment' when this action is launched.

▶ The most widely used JavaScript events are **onMouseOver** (when the cursor passes over a defined area), **onKeyPress** (when the user presses a key on the keyboard) and **onClick** (when the user clicks on a specified object). There are some thirty such events, most of which concern forms.

Note

HTML 4.0 has integrated these functions into the language, so they no longer need to be declared as JavaScript statements.

Because they can be used for such actions as 'when the mouse cursor passes over such and such a place on the page, such and such a function is triggered', events greatly enhance interactivity. Consequently, Web sites need no longer be static, but can be composed of pages that interact with the Net surfer.

Example 6

The following example illustrates events and control structures. Let's take a small questionnaire with the following question: 'In what year did the French Revolution take place?' When an OK-button is clicked (an **onClick** event), the value entered by the surfer is passed to a function that determines whether it is valid, by means of a conditional statement. If the answer is "1789", a message will inform the user that the answer is correct. Otherwise, another message will indicate that it's wrong, and will ask the user to try again.

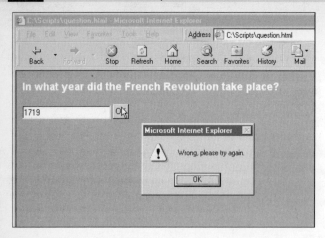

Here is the script for this example:

```
<FORM>
<P>In what year did the French Revolution take place?</P>
<INPUT TYPE= "text" VALUE="">
<INPUT TYPE= "button" VALUE= "OK"
```

```
        onClick="message(document.forms[0].
        elements[0].value)">
</FORM>


<SCRIPT LANGUAGE="JavaScript">


function message(date)
{ if (date=="1789")
        {alert("Correct!");
        }
   else
        {alert("Wrong, please try again.");
        }
}


</SCRIPT>
```

Syntax note

Note the use of the *strictly-equal operator* (==).
Note also that each of the statements following the
conditional clause and the **else** keyword is framed by
braces.

As in Example 3, an OK-button is associated with the
event **onClick**. Its argument is the answer entered by the
user in the text field. When the button is pressed (i.e. the
event occurs), the program invokes the function **message**(). This function checks the date entered against
"1789" and displays a message accordingly.

1.2. How to integrate JavaScript

Although this book is only an introduction to JavaScript
programming, the information it contains will enable
you to find ready-made scripts and to integrate them

with your pages. At the end of this chapter, we'll provide a number of such scripts that you can use. But you're undoubtedly aware there are countless such scripts on the Net, often freely available for you to use as you wish – a gigantic collection from which you can just pick out the choice morsels.

Obtaining a script is not enough, however. You must still be able to adapt it to your needs, and know how to integrate it with the code of your HTML pages. Most of the time, scripts downloadable from the Web will be accompanied by the information you need, at times on the site itself, at others in an attached file. But perhaps not every time …

Now that you've finished the first section, you should be able to find your way through the code of a script, and thus avoid making errors and losing precious time. Let's now see how to integrate your chosen script.

There are two ways to proceed:

1. Insert the script into the HTML code itself.

   This method uses a specific command to notify the browser that it is now dealing with JavaScript code and not HTML, so that it can interpret it accordingly. This command uses the tag pair <script> and </script>. But you must also specify the script language involved (JavaScript, VBScript, etc.):

   ```
   <SCRIPT LANGUAGE="JavaScript">
   ... the script code goes here ...
   </SCRIPT>
   ```

   The code is usually placed in the header of the HTML document, between the tags <HEAD> and </HEAD>. In some cases, however, the script must be contained in the body of the document, between the tags <BODY> and </BODY>. When a site offers scripts unencumbered by restrictions on usage, it usually provides such information as well.

2 Load the script via a link.

This procedure has a double advantage. Firstly, it means the JavaScript code doesn't take up space in your HTML document. Secondly, and above all, a link call saves you the trouble of multiple recopying when the same script is used several times on a Web site.

Proceed as follows:

```
<SCRIPT LANGUAGE="JavaScript"
     SRC="my_scripts/script1.js">

</SCRIPT>
```

my_scripts/script1.js is the access path of the script to be linked, and **.js** is the extension name of the JavaScript file.

This is relative addressing (i.e. relative to the address of the current page), but you can also use absolute addressing and specify the URL of the **.js** file:

```
<SCRIPT LANGUAGE="JavaScript"
     SRC="http://www.my_site/my_scripts/
     script1.js">
</SCRIPT >
```

The file containing the script is a simple text document saved with the extension **.js**. Note that it need not contain any **SCRIPT** declaration, as its extension already designates it as such.

1.3.   Compatibility

Everyone is aware nowadays of the keen competition between the two leading browsers on the market, Netscape Navigator and Microsoft Internet Explorer (IE). And the surfer is the first casualty of this browser war. It is up to Webmasters to provide compatible code, because otherwise some users will be deprived of part of the content of the sites they visit. And whereas some HTML tags are not supported in the same way by the two rivals, JavaScript suffers even more from incompatibility conflicts.

JavaScript was adopted by Netscape in Version 2 of its browser. Jscript is Microsoft's interpretation of JavaScript. It appeared with IE 3, was initially very close to the scripting language developed by Netscape, and featured similar functions. However, the gap gradually grew wider and new compatibility problems arose between the browsers, although a large subset of these two languages remains fully compatible. So how can you take full advantage of the functionality of scripts and ensure browser compatibility at the same time?

Several solutions are possible:

1 Provide a message notifying the visitor that the script will not run with the current browser. This option is useful if a visitor's browser is configured not to interpret scripts for security reasons.

Note: Script languages and security

Authorising the automatic execution of applications on your PC means exposing it to viruses. The recent 'I Love You' VBScript virus is a nasty case in point. That is why browsers offer several levels of security, including a prohibition on downloading active contents (such as JavaScript, Java or ActiveX).

As a precaution, it is a good idea to use the HTML containers **<NOSCRIPT>** and **</NOSCRIPT>**. Anything between these two tags will be ignored by a browser that can interpret the script, but will be displayed on the screen by the others.

It is also a good idea to use the comment tag-pair **<!--** and **// -->** to hide the code from browsers that do not recognise JavaScript. A script between these tags will also be visible in output from search engines on the Internet.

Example

```
<HEAD>
<SCRIPT LANGUAGE="JavaScript">
<!--

... Put your script code here ...

// -->
</SCRIPT>
</HEAD>

<BODY>
```

```
<NOSCRIPT>

Your browser will not run the scripts on this page.

</NOSCRIPT>
<BODY>
```

2 Use a browser-detection script and direct the visitor to a different page, depending on whether the browser is Netscape or Internet Explorer. This solution is the most laborious, as radically different code must at times be developed, but it is also the way to make your Web pages as generally available as possible. This script is provided in Chapter 3.2.

3 In some cases, tricks can be used to keep a single script for both browsers. We will try to use this option as much as possible.

1.4.   Debugging scripts

JavaScript is not as tolerant as HTML. A punctuation error, upper instead of lower case (or *vice versa*) or a forgotten parenthesis will cause the application to fail, often displaying a JavaScript error message. Debugging a script is often a hair-raising experience. To avoid such an unpleasant task, one rule of thumb is to **be careful with the syntax**, because it's responsible for most script errors. This book will enable you, initially at least, to integrate into your pages some of the freely-usable scripts you find on the Net and that you'll want to modify. Be very careful not to make any typing mistakes during this operation. And don't be in too great a hurry to define your own scripts – or if you are, then get a book on JavaScript that will give you more extensive syntax-related information.

Netscape and Microsoft have integrated tools with their respective browsers that can detect script errors on a Web page. These indicate the number of the line in the HTML code that contains an error, and a brief description of the cause.

Netscape has embedded a debugging console in its browser that displays script error messages accompanied by comments. You can access this console by typing **javascript:** in the browser address bar. (In Netscape 6, you access it via the **Tasks/Tools** menu instead.)

Netscape: Communicator Console

JavaScript Error: file:/Macintosh%20HD/Desktop%20Folder/Appl/Applet/temp.html, **line 21:**

t is not defined.
JavaScript Error: file:/Macintosh%20HD/Desktop%20Folder/Appl/Applet/temp.html, **line 26:**

t is not defined.
JavaScript Error: file:/Macintosh%20HD/Desktop%20Folder/Appl/Applet/temp.html, **line 39:**

fdgh is not defined.
JavaScript Error: file:/Macintosh%20HD/Desktop%20Folder/Appl/Applet/temp.html, **line 26:**

t is not defined.
JavaScript Error: file:/Macintosh%20HD/Desktop%20Folder/Appl/Applet/temp.html, **line 21:**

t is not defined.
JavaScript Error: file:/Macintosh%20HD/Desktop%20Folder/Appl/Applet/temp.html, **line 26:**

t is not defined.
JavaScript Error: file:/Macintosh%20HD/Desktop%20Folder/Appl/Applet/temp.html, **line 21:**

t is not defined.
JavaScript Error: file:/Macintosh%20HD/Desktop%20Folder/Appl/Applet/temp.html, **line 26:**

t is not defined.
JavaScript Error: file:/Macintosh%20HD/Desktop%20Folder/Appl/Applet/temp.html, **line 39:**

fdgh is not defined.
JavaScript Error: file:/Macintosh%20HD/Desktop%20Folder/Appl/Applet/temp.html, **line 26:**

t is not defined.

javascript typein

Clear Console   Close

Internet Explorer does not have this function, but an
alert-window displays similar information.

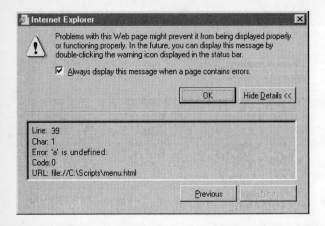

Finally, specialised debugging software packages are
available, such as Netscape JavaScript Debugger or
Microsoft Script Debugger from the browser manufac-
turers' Web sites.

1.5. Three JavaScript applications

The best way to get an idea of the depth and power of JavaScript is to visit Web sites devoted to it (a few addresses are in Appendix C). Here are some of the most widely used script applications. Three of them will be examined in detail presently.

▸ Mouseover effects (image replacement, link-colour change, etc.)

▸ Text effects (scrolling, display in the status bar, etc.)

▸ Use of forms

▸ Search engine

▸ Counters (number of visitors to a given site, for instance)

▸ Password

▸ Calculator

- Calendar or clock
- Buttons (close, back, next, etc.)

Rollover

The rollover is one of the most appreciated JavaScript applications: when the mouse rolls over an image, that image is replaced by another. This effect is used quite often to create animated buttons. Some WYSIWYG Web-page editors (for example, Dreamweaver) can create rollovers without your having to write the code yourself.

A rollover script uses an **onMouseOver/onMouseOut** pair of events. These may be associated with an image or a link, but the snag is that mouse events associated with an image, as in this case, are not recognised by Netscape Navigator, although they are OK with a link. You'll therefore have to rely on a trick to get round the compatibility problem.

Here is the code of the script:

```
<A HREF="javascript:void(0)"
  onMouseOver=document.images[0].src="over.jpg"
  onMouseOut=document.images[0].src="out.jpg">
<IMG SRC="out.jpg" border="0">
</A>
```

Comment

The link is rendered ineffective by means of the JavaScript operator **void**(0), which cancels an expression. All you have to do is to specify that this is a JavaScript command; otherwise, the browser would interpret it as an invalid address.

The first image is then inserted in the page (via the **IMG** tag). Here it is called **out.jpg**, but you can change it to that of your image (doing the same for the replacement image, of course).

The events **onMouseOver** and **onMouseOut** modify the source of the first image inserted in the document –

images[0]. Make sure you change this number if other images have been inserted higher up in the code of the page. The size of the border has been set to 0 to prevent it from appearing.

Note

To turn this rollover into a clickable button, all you have to do is to change **javascript:void**(0) to a valid link.

Note

The implementation of JavaScript by IE 3 does not recognise the **document.images** object. To avoid error messages for Internet users using this browser, it is advisable to make the execution of the script conditional:

```
if (document.images) {
// .... Put the JavaScript function here
}
```

An animated phrase

This script combines the opening of a pop-up window and a text-display effect. A phrase is displayed letter by letter. When all the characters have been displayed, the animation is reinitialised.

Here is the code of this script:

```
<HTML>
<HEAD>
<SCRIPT LANGUAGE="JavaScript">

function anim(letters)
{ pop.document.write("<BODY BGCOLOR='black'
TEXT='white'><H1>"+letters+"<H1>");
  pop.document.close();
  n++;
  if (n==20)
     {n=-10}
}

function go()
{ text=new String ("An animated phrase");
```

```
n=0;
pop=open("","","height=50, width=300");
setInterval("anim(text.substring(O,n))", 300);
}
```

```
</SCRIPT>
</HEAD>
```

```
<BODY onLoad="go()">
</BODY>
</HTML>
```

Comment

When the page is loaded (**<BODY onLoad="go()">**), the function **go()** is invoked. A character-string variable named **text** is declared by the statement **new String** (its value corresponds to a phrase that will be gradually displayed). A second variable (**n**) defines the number of characters of this phrase (initially 0). The method **open**() is then invoked.

This opens a pop-up window, to which we have given a name (**pop**) so that we can qualify it subsequently. Its properties are defined by arguments (separated by a comma without spaces). The first two are empty (they specify the URL to load and the name of the window), but the next two define the height and width of the window. A counter is then initialised using the method **setInterval**(), which takes two arguments. The first is a function call that will be repeated after an interval specified by the second argument (in our example, 300 milliseconds). We've named this function **anim**(). The parameter to it, which uses the method **substring**(), is a substring of our **text** string variable, beginning at character 0 (the start of the string) and ending at the nth character.

The function **anim**() displays this string in the pop-up window. The first time it is called, no character is displayed, because **n** is 0. **n** is then incremented, using the arithmetic increment operator **++**. The next time the function **anim**() is run, the number of displayed characters will be 1, the next time 2, and so forth. Once this number has exceeded the length of the chain text (and all characters are displayed), **n** will take the value −10. In this way, a small interval will elapse before the phrase reappears.

Note

The **document.close** statement closes the document opened in the pop-up window. Otherwise, a new extra line in the window would appear each time the function **anim**() was invoked.

Scrolling

In a Web page, text often takes up more space than is available on the screen. The user can read the hidden text by using the scrollbars.

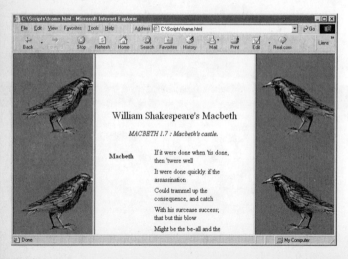

Scrolling, which is widely used in film credits, automates this process. Comfortable for the reader and visually more attractive than fixed text, scrolling offers an original reading solution.

The script code is as follows:

```
<HTML>
<HEAD>
<SCRIPT LANGUAGE="JavaScript">

var yposition = 0;

function scroll()
{ yposition++
  go(yposition)
}
```

```
function go(yposition)
{ scrollTo(0,yposition)
  setTimeout("scroll()",10)
}

setInterval("window.location.reload()",20000);

</SCRIPT>
</HEAD>

<BODY onLoad="scroll()">
<CENTER>
<P> </P>
<!—etc//–>
<P>first line of text </P>
<P>second line of text </P>
<!—etc//–>
```

```
<P> </P>
<!—etc//->
</CENTER>

</BODY>
</HTML>
```

Comment

Scrolling begins as soon as the Web page containing the text to be scrolled is downloaded (the event **onLoad** is used again).

What happens when the function **scroll**() is called because of this event?

[1] The variable **yposition**, defined in the script head (with a value of 0), is incremented, which will happen each time the function **scroll**() is invoked. In this way,

this variable guarantees continued scrolling until the end of the text is reached.

2 A second function, **go**(), is invoked in turn. The value of the variable **yposition** is passed to it as an argument.

3 The method **scrollTo**() is invoked by the function **go**(). A native method of the object window, it redefines the origin (the (x,y)-coordinates in relation to the upper left corner of the window) of the contents of a window (in our case, the text). The x-coordinate is set to 0 (scrolling here is vertical only), and the y-coordinate to the value of the variable **yposition**.

4 Once this new position is reached, one last method, **setTimeout**(), is used. This native JavaScript method is a timer. Unlike the case with **setInterval**(), the action specified as the first argument is launched only

once, after a certain period of time (specified by the second argument). The action to be repeated is of course the function **scroll**(), and the interval here is set at 10 milliseconds. So now we're all set to go again: a new value of **yposition** will go to the function **scroll**(), the text will be scrolled further, and so on.

Once the entire text has been scrolled, everything stops, as we have come to the end of the HTML document. But it would be convenient for the visitor to be able to read the text several times. To this end, we define a time interval after which the page will be reinitialised, as if the visitor had clicked the 'refresh' or 'reload' button on the browser. This interval depends on the length of the text, as we must wait for it to scroll entirely before reloading the page. So the last line of code in our script is:

```
setInterval("window.location.reload()",20000);
```

Here, **window.location** retrieves the URL of the current window, and **reload**() is the method that forces the browser to reload the page from this address. The numeric value that is the second argument to **setInterval**() corresponds to the time interval that we want to lapse between each repetition, expressed in milliseconds.

Note:

The body of the document contains the text to be scrolled. For the best visual effect, we've placed a series of blank lines before and after the text.

2. VBScript

VBScript (Visual Basic Script) is the script language developed by Microsoft to rival the JavaScript adopted by Netscape. With its syntax based largely on Visual Basic, it appeared for the first time with IE 3.0, albeit in a watered-down version.

VBScript and JavaScript have many similarities. They are both interpreted languages whose code is integrated into an HTML document. They are both geared to offering richer, more varied and more powerful functionality to Web pages.

In spite of its performance, VBScript is still less widespread than JavaScript, partly because Microsoft developed its own JavaScript implementation (Jscript), and partly for incompatibility reasons.

For this reason, our discussion of this language will be limited to this brief introduction.

3. Dynamic HTML

DHTML is a truly revolutionary development for creating Web pages. This technology makes it possible to access any constituent element or set of elements of an HTML page whatsoever; to edit the data and style; and to add behaviour, whether in terms of animation or interactivity. In a sentence, we can now escape the static state to which these components had doomed us up to now. It's possible, for instance, to enlarge the size of an image, change the colour of the text, move an object, replace a phrase with another or create a drop-down menu.

But DHTML is not a language in itself. It is actually a combination of HTML 4.0, script languages we have already discussed, and cascading style sheets.

3.1. | Cascading style sheets

Cascading style sheets (CSS) were created to separate the structure of an HTML document from its contents. They are used to specify the topographic styles of a Web page, without necessarily associating them with the elements that they format. Now, when the style is changed, all the elements affected by that style are changed as well. CSS applications make HTML formatting tags obsolete.

Declaring a style sheet

We'll now go over the various properties of style sheets.

There are three ways to declare a style sheet:

1. Directly in an HTML tag (on-line style) using the attribute **STYLE**.

Example

```
<P STYLE="text-align:center;font-size:24px;
color: blue">
   text here</P>
```

The keyword **STYLE** becomes associated with the HTML tag **<P>** (paragraph). Then comes the definition of the style proper (the presentation rule), placed between quotation marks. Each style attribute is separated by a semicolon, and its value is entered after a colon. Our example defines a new centred paragraph with a 24-pixel, blue font.

2 As a global style sheet defined in the header of the HTML file.

This will affect the entire document. The style is declared between the tags **<HEAD>** and **</HEAD>**, using the tag **<STYLE>** as a specific statement this time. The style type is indicated by the attribute **type="text/css"**. The presentation rules (style properties) are entered between braces and separated by semicolons.

Example

```
<HEAD>
<STYLE type="text/css">
P{text-align:center;font-size:18px}
H1{color:orange}
</STYLE>
</HEAD>
```

All characters entered between the tags **<P>** and **</P>** will henceforth be affected by the style defined in the header (central alignment, with a font size of

18 pixels). All **<H1>** headers will be displayed in an orange font.

We can also attribute presentation rules to a named style, or class. This name is then used instead of a set of HTML attributes.

Example

<HEAD>

<STYLE TYPE="text/css">

.mystyle{font-family:sans-serif;font-size:12px;color: lightblue}

</STYLE>

</HEAD>

A class is always preceded by a dot (.). It can hence-forth be associated with any element in the body of the document, using the tag **CLASS**:

```
<P class="mystyle">text here</P>
```

3. By a link to an external style sheet ('linked' style sheets).

Style sheets are simple text files with the extension .css. The link is invoked in the header of the document by means of the following tag:

```
<LINK TYPE="text/css" REL="stylesheet"
href="mystyle.css">
```

This command needs little comment: **REL** specifies that the linked element is a style sheet and **mystyle.css** indicates the address (absolute or relative) of the style sheet to be linked.

Dynamic positioning

In addition to adding style functionality, CSS provide positioning properties for the different components of an HTML document. This syntax is called CSS-P, for CSS Positioning.

Using HTML alone, elements can be given only a statically-aligned position, one that is specified relative to the browser window. Quite complex operations with tables are often needed to make the most of these limited possibilities.

CSS-P properties define three types of positioning: static, relative and absolute. An element displayed in absolute position is extracted from the flow of the document and becomes completely independent of it. Numerous sites use the properties of CSS-P, although this may not be visible.

The positioning coordinates are given as x- and y-values, but also – and this is a major contribution of DHTML – in terms of depth (i.e. z-values). This means that each element can occupy a different plane, and be superimposed on the others. The principle is similar to the layer management offered by graphic software packages such as PhotoShop and Flash.

Finally, the visibility property defines whether or not an element will be visible.

Some CSS-P properties:

▸ **Name or id:** This is the name associated with an element or group of elements when its properties are declared.

▸ **Position:** This can be static (the default), relative or absolute.

▸ **Top, left:** These properties, expressed in pixels and applicable to any positioning element, absolute or relative, specify the coordinates of the top left point of an element.

▸ **Height, width:** These define the height and width of a layer in relation to the left border of the page, expressed in pixels.

- **Background:** This defines the background colour.

- **Clip:** This property takes as its value the keyword **rect**, for clipping rectangle. Any object outside this rectangle will be invisible. The coordinates of the rectangle are entered between parentheses, separated by spaces and specified in the following order: top right bottom left (see Chapter 3.2, 'Fading effect').

- **Visibility:** This specifies whether the element is visible or hidden.

- **Z-index:** This property determines the position of an object on the z-axis. The object with the highest z index is at the top.

- **Overflow:** This describes how to display any absolute position element that overflows the area allotted to it through the properties height, width or clip.

Domain Object Model

The Domain Object Model (DOM) is the syntax used to access HTML objects and to manipulate them through scripting languages. We have seen how an object is extracted from a document flow (CSS and CSS-P). We can now access it and entrust it to the magical powers of JavaScript (or another scripting language). Unfortunately, in spite of the efforts of Committee W3C, no standard has yet been defined for DOM. And, once again, there are many differences between the Netscape and Microsoft methods. In many cases, specific code must be developed for each browser.

Layers: the Netscape implementation

Netscape has opted to create a new object called a *layer*, on which the dynamic positioning properties are applied. The new container tags (not recognised by Internet Explorer) used to define a layer are **<LAYER>** and

</LAYER>. All elements contained by the layer are inserted between these two tags. For optimal implementation, CSS-P properties under Netscape should be declared using the tag **<LAYER>**. Nevertheless, to avoid a specific declaration for each browser, the approach based on style sheets implemented by Microsoft can be used (see next paragraph). Some properties are recognised by Netscape and require a specific declaration using the tag **<LAYER>**.

The properties of a layer are accessed by calling them by name, qualified according to the syntax shown in this example:

document.layers[n].property

Here, **n** represents the number of the layer in order of appearance within the document.

To modify a property, you simply change the value. For example:

document.layers[n].top="200"

Document.all: the Microsoft implementation

Microsoft has remained closer to style sheets and has not created a new tag specifically for integrating the CSS-P.

An object is accessed by the keywords **document.all**, which designate everything contained in a document. The object is then qualified by its name or according to its order of appearance in the document, as we have already seen in the chapter devoted to JavaScript.

Declaration of a group of objects

To apply an absolute position to a text or a group of objects, the tags **<DIV>** and **</DIV>** are used. All elements contained between these two tags are considered to form a single object. The properties of a set of elements are declared by means of the attribute **<STYLE>**.

Example:

```
<BODY bgColor="gray">
<DIV id="w3c" style="position:absolute;
    color:darkblue; background:white; height:140;
    width:320; top:100; left:100;
    z-index:1; visibility:visible">
<CENTER>
<BR>
<P>The World Wide Web consortium (W3C) develops
interoperable technologies (specifications, guidelines,
software, and tools) to lead the Web to its full potential
as a forum for information, commerce, communication,
and collective understanding.</P>
<IMG src="logo.gif" border=0>
<P><A HREF="www.w3.org">Click here
to visit the Web site</A></P>
<BR>
</CENTER>
</DIV>
</BODY>
</HTML>
```

The 'layer' created above comprises a paragraph, an image and a link.

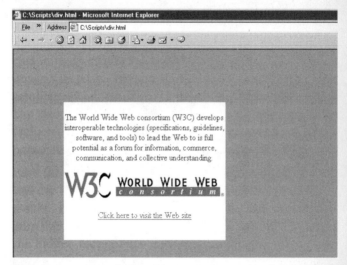

The properties of an element are accessed by name, using the syntax:

Document.all.my_layer:property

To modify a property, you simply change the value.

Example:
----
document.all.mylayer.top="200"

3.2. Three DHTML applications

Here, the Web is once again a crucible for you to use. For example, here are some of the most widely used DHTML applications:

▸ Text animations – moving titles, rotating banners …

▸ Image animations – scrolling, fading, layering …

▸ Menus – navigation bars, drop-down menus …

▸ Tooltips

▸ Games – Hangman …

In short, DHTML does everything that JavaScript can do, and gives you the further possibilities made available through layers.

Note

The most sophisticated HTML editors (Dreamweaver, GoLive, Namo Web Editor, etc.) offer WYSIWYG solutions for creating DHTML animations.

Before we delve into the heart of the matter, let's examine a simple means for identifying the browser when downloading a Web page, so as to guide the visitor to the appropriate page.

Detecting the browser

```
<HTML>
<HEAD>
<SCRIPT LANGUAGE="JavaScript">

function detect()
{ if (navigator.appName=="Netscape")
        {this.location="pageNetscape.html"
        }
  else
        {this.location="pageIE.html"
        }
}


</SCRIPT>
</HEAD>
```

```
<BODY onLoad="detect()">
</BODY>
</HTML>
```

This script is placed at the head of the home page (most of the time the page contained in the file 'index.html') and activated when the page is downloaded (**onLoad**). It accesses the property **appName** of the object **navigator**. This property specifies the name of the browser as a character string: "Netscape" for Netscape Communicator and "Internet Microsoft Explorer" for IE. The function **detect**() accesses this property and replaces the current URL (**this.location**) by the appropriate browser-related address.

Another way of doing this would be to create variables that consist of appropriate statements for Netscape or Explorer, as follows. We first define a boolean variable **navi** that compares the character string value of the object **navigator.appName** against "Netscape":

Var navi= (navigator.appName == "Netscape")

Other variables are then declared, the value of which depend on the truth-value of **navi**. The general syntax of this declaration is:

```
If (navi)
 {var = "first_value";
 }
else
 {layer = "first_value";
 }
```

Drop-down menu

Creating a drop-down menu is one of the most useful DHTML interactive applications. The principle consists of displaying a menu so that, when the mouse passes over one of its elements, a submenu drops down to show several new options. Each option is a link. When the mouse cursor moves away, the submenu disappears.

To create such a menu, CSS-P positioning and visibility properties must be used. All menus and submenus are then presented on the page, but only the main menu is visible at the outset. To show the submenus, we use the event **onMouseOver**.

Developing the script

The first step consists of creating the various menus and submenus. We could limit ourselves to simple textual links, but graphics provide greater variety.

Let's consider a main menu formed of three juxtaposed tabs, 170 pixels wide and 52 pixels high. We'll differentiate them by their names. Each tab drops down as the mouse passes over, and shows a submenu composed of several links. To simplify the code, the submenu in our example has only one link, but the principle should be clear.

```
<HTML>
<HEAD>
<SCRIPT LANGUAGE="javascript">

var navi= (navigator.appName == "Netscape")

if (navi)
{ layer = "document.layers";
  style = ""
}
else
{ layer = "document.all";
  style = ".style"
}

function show (smenu)
{ eval(layer + '["' + smenu + '"]' + style + '.visibility="visible"');
}
```

```
function hide(smenu)
{ eval(layer + '["' + smenu + '"]' + style + '.visibility=
    "hidden"');
}


</SCRIPT>
</HEAD>
<BODY bgcolor="#9E9E9E">


<TABLE border=0 cellspacing=0 cellpadding=0 cols=3>
<TR align=center>
  <TD width="220">
    <A href="javascript:void(0)"
      onMouseOver="document.images[0].src=
          'menu1on.gif', show('smenu1')"
      onMouseOut="document.images[0].src=
          'menu1off.gif', hide('smenu1')">
```

```
<IMG src="menu1off.gif" border=0 height= 52
  width=170>
</A>
</TD>

<TD width="220">
  <A href="javascript:void(O)"

    onMouseOver="document.images[1].src=
      'menu2on.gif',show('smenu2')">

    onMouseOut="document.images[1].src=
      'menu2off.gif',hide('smenu2')">

  <IMG src="menu2off.gif" border=0
    height=52 width=170>
  </A>
</TD>

<TD width="220">
  <A href="javascript:void(O)"
```

```
    onMouseOver="document.images[2].src='menu3on.gif',
        show('smenu3')"
    onMouseOut ="document.images[2].src='menu3off.gif',
        hide('smenu3')">
  <IMG src="menu3off.gif" border=0 height=
      52 width=170>
  </A>
 </TD>
</TR>
</TABLE>

<DIV id="smenu1" style="position:absolute; top:60;
    left:10; z-index:1;visibility:hidden">
  <A href="link1.html" onMouseOver="show('smenu1')",
                    onMouseOut="hide('smenu1')">
  <IMG src="smenu1on.gif" border=0>
  </A>
</DIV>
```

```
<DIV id="smenu2" style="position:absolute; top:60;
   left:230;z-index:1; visibility:hidden">
  <A href="link2.html" onMouseOver="show('smenu2')",
                    onMouseOut="hide('smenu2')">
  <IMG src="smenu2on.gif" border=0>
  </A>
</DIV>


<DIV id="smenu3" style="position:absolute; top:60;
   left:450;z-index:1; visibility:hidden">
  <A href="link3.html" onMouseOver="show('smenu3')",
                    onMouseOut="hide('smenu3')">
  <IMG src="smenu3on.gif" border=0>
  </A>
</DIV>


</BODY>
</HTML>
```

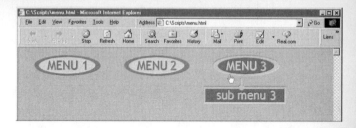

Comment

Let's start with the body of the page – a table composed of three cells, with the images of the main menu still visible. The events **onMouseOver** and **onMouseOut** when the mouse rolls over the image of each menu tab will invoke the functions **show**() and **hide**(), which will show or hide the various submenus. The submenus are then declared by means of the tag **<DIV>**. They are placed in an absolute position precisely at the location where they will be shown, and declared invisible. The menus are floated thanks to having a z-coordinate value higher than that of the (main) menu, which proves particularly useful if they are superimposed on certain elements of the background layer.

The script itself first defines variables for accessing the properties of the submenus according to the Netscape and Microsoft syntax, as the case may be (see Chapter 3.1). The functions **show**() and **hide**() are child's play, as they simply show and hide the submenu. Only the syntactical differences between Netscape and Explorer complicate these functions, because they require juggling with the concatenation operator **+** and quotation marks. The concatenation will be carried out by the function **eval**() (which 'evaluates' the character string used as argument), and the visibility property is set as either visible or hidden.

Fading effect

DHTML offers a wide variety of effects that can be applied to text and images by tinkering with positioning, visibility, clipping, colour and other such properties. The fade-in/fade-out effect, so prized by the cinema, offers an original solution for image transition.

The principle is simple. Two images of the same size are superimposed, but a clipping rectangle with zero width is applied on the top image. As everything that overflows from this rectangle is invisible, the image is completely hidden. The width is then incremented repetitively, gradually revealing the image below.

```
<HTML>
<HEAD>
<SCRIPT LANGUAGE="JavaScript">


var navi = (navigator.appName == "Netscape");
w=0;


function fade()
{ if (navi)

    {document.image3.visibility='show';

     document.image3.clip.right=w}

  else

    {document.all.image2.style.clip='rect(0 '+
    w +' 250 0)'};

w++;

time=setTimeout("fade()", 5);
```

```
if (w == 300)
  {clearTimeout(time)}
}

function hideimage()
{ if (!navi)
    {document.all.image4.style.visibility='hidden'}
}


</SCRIPT>
</HEAD>
<BODY bgcolor="gray" onLoad="hideimage()">

<FORM>
  <INPUT TYPE="button" VALUE="fade"
      onClick="fade()">
</FORM>
```

```
<DIV ID="image1" style="position:absolute; top:40;
       left:10;z-index:0; visibility:visible">
  <IMG src="image1.jpg" border=0>
</DIV>


<DIV ID="image2" style="position:absolute; top:40;
       left:10;z-index:1; overflow:hidden;
       visibility:visible;clip:'rect( 0 0 250 0)'">
  <IMG src="image2.jpg" border=0>
</DIV>


<LAYER ID="image3" z-index="1" left="10" top="40"
       visibility="hide">
  <IMG ID="image4" src="image2.jpg" border=0>
</LAYER>


</BODY>
</HTML>
```

This script requires little if any further comment. All the functions it uses have already been dealt with in this book.

Text scrolling

This script capitalises once again on the dynamic positioning properties which, combined with JavaScript counters, can animate any object. In this example, we create two blocks of text, each consisting of several words. These two text blocks are combined to form a phrase. When the page opens, the blocks are invisible because they are situated outside the screen – the first on the left, the second on the right. The function **move**() activated when the page is loaded will change the position of these two elements by incrementing the x position of the left block by 5 pixels (**left** property), and decreasing that of the right block. This function is repeated by a counter (**setTimeout**()), which is cancelled when the elements have reached their final position.

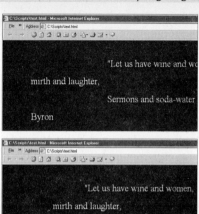

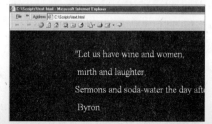

```
<HTML>
<HEAD>
<STYLE TYPE="text/css">

.text1{position:absolute; top:50; left:-500; width:1000;
     font-size:28px;color:white; z-index:0}

.text2{position:absolute; top:50; left:-1000;width:1000;
     font-size:28px; color:white; z-index:1}
</STYLE>

<SCRIPT LANGAGE="javascript">

var navi=(navigator.appName == "Netscape");
w=1000;
v=-600;

function move()
{
w=w-2;
v=v+2;
```

```
if (navi)
    {document.layers["text1"].left=w;
    document.layers["text2"].left=v;
    }
else
    {
    document.all.text1.style.left=w;
    document.all.text2.style.left=v;
    }
time=setTimeout("move()", 5);
if(v==204)
    {clearTimeout(time);
    }
}

</SCRIPT>
</HEAD>
<BODY bgColor="black"; onLoad="move()">
<DIV ID="text1" class="text1">
<P>"Let us have wine and women,</P>
<P> </P>
```

```
<P>Sermons and soda-water the day after."</P>
</DIV>

<DIV ID="text2" class="text2">
<P> </P>
<P>mirth and laughter,</P>
<P> </P>
<P>Byron</P>
</DIV>

</BODY>
</HTML>
```

PART II

The animated multimedia Web

4. Java applets and ActiveX

Java applets and ActiveX are multimedia technologies (concerned with animation and interactivity) and controllers of multimedia objects. As multimedia technologies, they are used to create applications that are similar to scripts but far more powerful (such as warping of text or an image, 3D graphics, etc.). As controllers they behave like plug-ins and boost the browser's functionality.

4.1. Java applets

The term *applet* means 'small application'. It's usually associated with Java, though not exclusively.

Developed by Sun Microsystems, Java is an object-oriented language used to write programs that are compiled as applets on Web pages and interpreted by the browser. The browser uses a *Java virtual machine* to execute the code. This software component is in principle available on all computers, irrespective of the operating system and hardware architecture. So in addition to being powerful, Java has the great advantage of being universal.

The drawback of Java is that it is slow. Because they require substantial resources, Java applets should be used in a Web page only with care. Nevertheless, although Java may not be the only language that could be used to create applications, applets can come in very handy for Web site designers, who don't need to know the intricacies of programming, but can just insert them ready-made into a page.

Inserting an applet into a Web page

The Net is teeming with Java applets. They can be downloaded from many sites, where they are often arranged by topic and usually accompanied by a help file. A list of some of these sites is in Appendix C.

An applet is inserted into a Web page by means of a specific content tag, **<APPLET>**. The applet itself is identified by its name, followed by the extension **.class** (all between quotation marks, although this is optional in recent browsers and in recent versions of HTML).

Examples

```
<APPLET code="applet52.class"></APPLET>
```

An applet will most often request that space be set aside so that it can display something on the screen. So its size must also be indicated:

```
<APPLET code="applet52.class" width=100
     height=40></APPLET>
```

All this assumes that the applet **applet52.class** is in the same folder as the HTML document in which it is integrated. Otherwise, the folder containing the applet must be specified by means of the keyword **codebase**:

```
<APPLET codebase="applets" code="applet52.class"
     width=100 height=40></APPLET>
```

This example uses relative addressing, but you can use an absolute address instead.

The tag OBJECT

HTML 4.0 introduced a new generic tag for inserting any external program or multimedia object (via a plug-in or another specific application). Such an object can be an image, a sound, a video sequence, ActiveX, an applet and so on. The tag establishes not only a standard method for including different types of existing media, but also handles the integration of other objects in the future, which will no longer require specific tags.

This command makes previous tags such as **<APPLET>**, **<IMG>** and **<EMBED>** obsolete, although they are still supported by current browsers. On the other hand, it is far more complicated to use than its predecessors and is not yet fully supported by various browsers.

With some 25 attributes, this tag at times requires meticulous programming, the syntax of which may vary depending on the object. Therefore, although we advise you to consider using it, we won't go into the attributes here. For more information, visit the W3C site at *www.w3.org*.

Positioning an applet on a Web page

An applet is inserted into a page in the same way as for any other HTML object. The usual positioning tags therefore apply here as elsewhere.

Example

```
<APPLET codebase="applets" code="applet52.class"
     width=100 height=40 align=middle
     vspace=50 hspace=50></APPLET>
```

Applet settings

Although the user need not know the code of the applet (which is here compiled in the file 'applet52.class'), some settings are probably needed to run it and must be customised. Examples might include the URL of an image, its size, the background or font colour, the scrolling speed, etc. The tag we use is **<PARAM>**, which has two attributes: **name** (parameter name) and **value** (value attributed to the name). So the general form of the parameter is: **<param name=XXX value=YYY>**.

Let's take the example of an applet (developed by Dolf van der Schaar) that generates a browser menu in 3D as a cube. Each face of the cube is a link, and the accompanying comment is shown below the cube. To access the hidden faces of the cube, you use the mouse to turn it in space.

Although there are many parameters, they're very easy to change.

Here is the code to slot into an HTML file to add a 3D menu – you'll want to change some of the parameter values to suit your own needs, of course:

```
<APPLET code="menu3D.class" width=200 height=200>

<PARAM NAME="CUBESIZE" VALUE="100">
<PARAM NAME="FACTOR" VALUE="150">
<PARAM NAME="I0" VALUE="face1.gif">
<PARAM NAME="I1" VALUE="face2.gif">
```

```
<PARAM NAME="I2" VALUE="face3.gif">
<PARAM NAME="I3" VALUE="face4.gif">
<PARAM NAME="I4" VALUE="face5.gif">
<PARAM NAME="I5" VALUE="face6.gif">
<PARAM NAME="I0A" VALUE="1">
<PARAM NAME="I1A" VALUE="1">
<PARAM NAME="I2A" VALUE="1">
<PARAM NAME="I3A" VALUE="1">
<PARAM NAME="I4A" VALUE="1">
<PARAM NAME="I5A" VALUE="1">
<PARAM NAME="REF0" VALUE=
"http://www.link1.html">
<PARAM NAME="REF1" VALUE=
"http://www.link2.html">
<PARAM NAME="REF2" VALUE=
"http://www.link3.html">
<PARAM NAME="REF3" VALUE=
"http://www.link4.html">
```

```
<PARAM NAME="REF4" VALUE=
"http://www.link5.html">

<PARAM NAME="REF5" VALUE=
"http://www.link6.html">

<PARAM NAME="BACKCOLOR" VALUE="000000">

<PARAM NAME="TEXT0" VALUE="LINK 1">

<PARAM NAME="TEXT1" VALUE="LINK 2">

<PARAM NAME="TEXT2" VALUE="LINK 3">

<PARAM NAME="TEXT3" VALUE="LINK 4">

<PARAM NAME="TEXT4" VALUE="LINK 5">

<PARAM NAME="TEXT5" VALUE="LINK 6">

</APPLET>
```

Where:

- ▶ CUBESIZE is the size of the cube's edges in pixels.

- ▶ FACTOR is the cube perspective distortion factor (the value can range between 100 for not distorted and 999 for very distorted).

- ▶ I0 to I5 specify the (relative) address of the images of each of the cube's six faces. We've replaced the existing images with the faces of a die, by modifying them one by one in Photoshop.

- ▶ I0A to I5A determine the number of constituent frames of each of the images in .gif format. So it's possible to use an animated GIF for each face of the cube (see Chapter 6).

- ▶ REF0 to REF5 are absolute Web addresses to be used as links.

▸ BACKCOLOR is the hexadecimal value of the background colour (black in our example).

▸ TEXT0 to TEXT5 are the character strings that will be shown under the cube as the mouse passes over each face.

As you can see, the many parameters of this applet in no way make it more complicated to use.

Although parameters to applets that you can download from the Net are not always fully explained, you'll usually be able to guess their meaning and change them as you wish without any difficulty.

Note

A similar applet can be downloaded in a shareware kit of 40 applets (Anfy 1.4) from *www. anfyteam.com*

Software solutions

Some software packages enable you to create Java applets without having to enter a single line of code. Most are usually devoted to creating buttons, menus and navigation bars, but you can also find applications for creating visual effects on images or text.

We'll single out here two small shareware applications that are easy to use and whose names describe exactly what they do: Applet Effects Factory and Applet Button Factory, from CoffeeCup Software (*www.coffeecup.com*).

▸ Applet Effects Factory features a range of 20 effects for images, including transition filters (fading, flipping, etc.) or viewing filters (noise, zoom, play on colours, rotation, waves, etc.). The latter can be applied to a single image or to a sequence of images.

▸ Applet Button Factory is slightly more complicated, but also extremely sophisticated. Briefly, a large number of available button samples can be modified completely (so that you can change their colour, background image, font, transparency, etc.), integrating events such as onLoad, onMouseOver and onClick, adding a text field to describe the link, or associating them with sound files! You can also insert your own graphics (buttons or background images) in GIF or JPEG format.

Example of a menu with an 'onMouseOver' event on the first button.

Commercial software applications worth mentioning include 1 Cool Button Tool (*www.buttontool.com*) and Auscomp eNavigator suite (*www.auscomp.com*). These user-friendly WYSIWYG applications can be used to create buttons, rollovers, navigation or pop-up menus, small animations, etc.

4.2. ActiveX

ActiveX is a set of Internet and multimedia technologies originally developed by Microsoft for Internet Explorer 3.0. Embedded in an HTML page, ActiveX components are used in many applications such as when incorporating a composite object that maintains a link with the application that created it (ActiveX documents), controlling such an object (ActiveX controls), supporting script languages (ActiveX Scripting) or managing external programs (ActiveX Server Framework). They also make it possible for Web pages to avail themselves of all the functionality of Windows. To sum up, ActiveX is a competitor of Java. Programmed in C or Visual Basic, ActiveX components can be compared to Java applets and are integrated and parameterised in an HTML page in the same way (using tags such as **OBJECT**, **EMBED** and **PARAM**).

Unlike Java, however, ActiveX is not a multi-platform technology. Whereas it can be embedded in the Mac OS as a plug-in, the integration is limited and does not extend to other systems such as Linux. According to certain statistics, there is one ActiveX component for every 50 Java applets used on the Net. Because we are limiting ourselves here to technologies that are widely compatible, we'll confine ourselves to these few introductory remarks.

5. Video on the Web

Sometimes the Web seems to fall far short of its prom-
ise. The widespread belief that the Internet is a true
multimedia environment makes one wonder. Video
sequences are rare, furtive and halting. And they are so
small that they could easily be viewed on a six-inch
screen.

The explanation lies in the very foundations of the
Internet; for its main purpose is communication and
data interchange. Transfer protocols may well become
ever more extensive, but the Net is always saturated, and
data downloading is way too slow. On this front, video
is a real juggernaut. Whereas an e-mail or a page of text
runs to a few kilobytes and an image to a few tens of
kilobytes, a video is always in the megabyte range.
That's why video must always be a little skinny. And
even then it has to be compressed, with quantity con-
siderations taking precedence over quality. A video still
takes much longer to download than to view. One

widely used solution for excessively large files is to download them in a compressed format (zipped). But then they usually cannot be viewed in real time, though *streamed* real-time formats such as RealVideo are now becoming available (see later).

However, we should not despair. The Internet is still in its infancy and is bound to surprise us. We must also admit that some innovations have already changed the face of multimedia beyond recognition on the Net.

5.1. Video formats

The diversity of formats that is so characteristic of multimedia applies to video as well. Each video software system has its own native format, and the performance race is constantly giving rise to new technologies that extend this variety even more.

Some standards have nonetheless emerged and are today integrated in the various operating systems. And consequently, such files can be read by multimedia players and browsers.

To view a file coded in a non-standard format, you'll need a *plug-in*. This is a small ancillary program that, as its name implies, is plugged into an application (your browser, in this case) and boosts its functionality. When a data format becomes very successful, it is frequently integrated into the next version of the browser, and becomes a new standard.

The most widely used formats are:

AVI (.avi)

Audio Video Interleave is the Windows standard. Not very compressed, it provides sequences that are of good quality but large in size. It is used frequently on the Net, often for very short sequences.

MPEG (.mpg)

Based on the JPEG compression standard, this format, developed by the Moving Pictures Experts Group, provides a good trade-off against file size. This has made it the standard for DVD and for many digital cameras. It includes a large number of offshoots, the most widely used on the Web being MPEG2 (MPEG Player 2).

QuickTime (.qt) and Movie (.mov)

QuickTime is the Macintosh standard which, adapted for Windows, has led to the .mov format. Although it offers quite good quality, it is slow to download. QuickTime 3 features streaming functions.

RealMedia (.rm)

RealMedia combines two formats that were originally different, RealVideo and RealAudio. They both feature *streaming* technology, and a compression rate that can lead to file sizes one-fifth that of the equivalent AVI files. The advantage of streaming has made it one of the most popular formats on the Internet, although the quality is not always up to par. Recently, thanks to RealVideo and QuickTime, the dream of television on-line is apparently close to becoming reality.

Note: Streaming

Streaming allows you to play a file (sound or video) without having to wait for it to finish downloading. Instead, the file is downloaded in small packages. In streaming, the file begins to be played as soon as the first package is downloaded, and then continues piece by piece. The streaming is ensured by using *buffering*, in which data is read ahead of being played. When bytestream fluctuations occur, as they frequently do on the Net, the missing or delayed data may be found in this buffer zone. The most widely used formats that feature this technology are RealVideo from Real Networks, QuickTime from Apple, Windows Media from Microsoft and Shockwave from Macromedia.

5.2. Playing video clips

With the exception of RealVideo, all the formats mentioned so far are supported by the latest versions of Windows Media Player for Windows and QuickTime Player for Macintosh; the latter is also available in a

Windows version. When a video sequence is selected on a Web page, the player is activated and downloading begins. A dialogue box then asks you whether you want to open the file on-line or to save it to disk. In both cases, you have to wait for the file to finish downloading before you can view the sequence, unless it is in streaming format.

Playing RealMedia sequences requires RealPlayer, one version of which is available free of charge from *www.real.com/player/index.html*. There is also a Pro version with much greater functionality that costs around £20.

5.3. Encoding

To create your own animated sequences, you will of course need video recording equipment (such as a camera, *Webcam* or digital camera). An analogue source will have to be digitised through a video acquisition card. Initially for professionals only, these cards are increasingly becoming affordable by more and more users (currently at around £100). Digital cameras usually encode data into AVI or MPEG formats.

Juggling with various formats depends on the software, and we won't go into all the procedures, which are as many and varied as the software applications themselves. We should nonetheless mention Adobe Première (an application for digitising films), Mac QuickTime 3 Pro and Windows Media Encoder.

We will, however, discuss encoding in RealMedia format, which can be easily handled, free of charge, with RealProducer.

This is available from *www. realnetworks.com/products/ producer/info.html*, and is a skeletal but perfectly functional version of RealProducer Plus (which costs about £100).

How to proceed

Encoding procedures depend on the video source (analogue or digital) and on the result you want (quality, scope of audience, type of integration in a Web page, standard server or Real Networks RealServer, etc.). Application *wizards* guide you step by step through the encoding process.

Amongst all these different methods, we've chosen to describe in detail how you can encode a video file on your hard disk and insert it into a Web page. RealProducer and its various wizards will show you how the other encoding procedures work.

When you launch the program, a new coding session starts with a choice of three solutions:

▸ Encode from a file on your hard disk. This would have an extension .avi or .mov.

▸ Encode from a sequence extracted from a multimedia device, such as a CD player or a digital camera.

▸ Download the file online from a RealServer.

1. Select the first choice and press **OK**. In the next window, you can identify the source of the file to be encoded in .rm format. Click **Next**.

3. Now enter information about your sequence: title, author, copyright, description and keywords. (Keywords will be helpful when you're searching for this page in the future.) Once you've completed these fields, click **Next**.

3. The next stage requires a word of explanation. As you know, a sequence is played image by image. For a video clip to be screened smoothly, images must be loaded at a certain rate (24 per second at the cinema, at least 12 per second in a cartoon); otherwise the picture will be jerky. Furthermore, the transfer rate must be fast enough to keep up with this bytestream

– you can't have streaming if the relevant information hasn't yet arrived! The transfer rate depends on the type of connection (standard modem, ADSL line, cable, etc.). The more restricted the connection, the less the quantity of data transmitted in a given time. Images will have to be smaller and of lower resolution – therefore more compressed, and ultimately of inferior quality.

In our case, we must define the type of audience (i.e. the type of connection) for which our sequence is intended. If we choose a low bytestream rate (e.g. a 28.8 kbps modem), the clip will be accessible by all, but the image will be of mediocre quality. On the other hand, a sequence encoded for an audience with a transfer rate of 200 kilobytes per second (ASDL) will be of very good quality, but a person viewing through a standard modem connection will find the picture jerky.

4. The window on your screen has several encoding options that will adjust the quality of the sequence to the type of connection used. The first option (Sure Streaming) is available only with the Pro version of the software, so you must go with the second choice, i.e. encoding based on a single rate.

5. The best compromise is to select a 56K modem, which is still the average connection rate amongst users. Although you must not expect miracles in terms of quality, you can rest assured that most of your audience will enjoy the full benefits of streaming.

6. In the next window, you can adjust the quality of the image to the action speed of the sequence. The faster the action, the more likely it is that the quality of the image will suffer, and the streaming trip up.

7. Finally, select the directory in which to save your **.rm** file.

8 Click **Next** to get a summary of the file's characteristics. These are shown in the main window of RealProducer which is now on your screen.

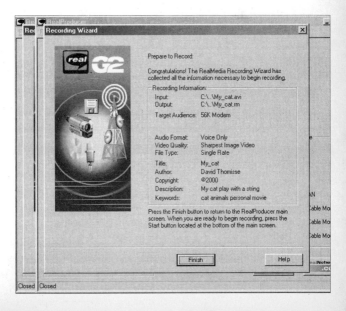

9 Click the **Start** button at the bottom of the window to start the encoding process, the progress of which will be indicated by the progress bar at the bottom right.

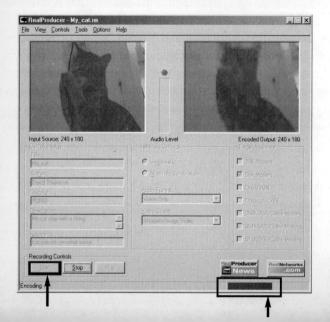

Once the encoding has been completed, your **.rm** file is ready, and you can now insert it into your Web page. RealProducer has a wizard that automates this process. You can create a Web page and insert a Real sequence, and publish it on the Web using the RealProducer FTP module. Remember, however, that only servers equipped with RealServer can broadcast your sequence in streaming mode – unless you use HTTP streaming, which is a possibility if your site will not be saturated with visitors.

In principle, a RealMedia sequence should be published by a server equipped with the RealServer software. The URL of the sequence calls on the Streaming server, which takes charge of its distribution. Streaming is then more efficient and adapts to the connection rate of the user. However, for a site that is limited in scope (containing few sequences and generating little traffic), the streaming HTTP solution is quite satisfactory and much more sensible.

Note

Note that creating a Web page automatically with RealProducer has two drawbacks:

▸ Firstly, it will only work if your page is still blank, because it will overwrite existing information.

▸ Secondly, in inserting the sequence, it adds other elements as well (such as a logo) that take up sizeable space on your page, although you can remove them manually afterwards.

5.4. Inserting a video sequence into a Web page

Most WYSIWYG Web page editors allow you to insert a video sequence into a Web page without having to enter any code. The standard formats are supported, and you can adjust the control properties such as the length of the sequence, loop repetition or the type of controllers available. Although this method is fast and easy to use, it is not always reliable, nor are all the aforementioned formats always supported.

Inserting a video sequence using HTML code, on the other hand, is no simple matter because of the diversity of formats and their handling by different browsers, including the way they manage the HTML tags concerned.

There are two ways to insert a video sequence in a page:

1. The first, the easier and more reliable of the two, is to use a link to the sequence. When this link is activated, the browser launches the downloading procedure. When the download is complete, the sequence is played by the relevant multimedia player.

Example

```
<A HREF="my_film.mpg">Click to view my sequence
(Mpeg, 500 kb)</A>
```

2. The second method consists of "loading" the sequence from the page itself, as if it were an image. You can then specify which controllers will be displayed, create the graphics, etc. But this comes at a price: compatibility. There are several HTML tags:

- DYNSRC – Used as an attribute of the IMG tag, it specifies the URL of the file to be embedded. Unfortunately, this tag is not recognised by Netscape, so we will not delve further into it.

- OBJECT – See Chapter 4.1.

- EMBED – Specific to multimedia elements, this tag uses plug-ins that enable the browser to manage the different objects that can be viewed in a Web page. It is quite simple to use, and is compatible with all browsers (in particular IE3). An alternative text or image can be placed between the tags **<NOEMBED>** and **</NOEMBED>**.

  The main attributes of the **EMBED** tag are:

  - **ALIGN**: specifies the control alignment (right, left, top, bottom).

  - **WIDTH** and **HEIGHT**: define the console size (in pixels).

- **SRC**: designates the URL of the file.

- **CONTROLLER** (true or false): specifies whether the control panel of the console is displayed (true by default).

- **AUTOSTART** (true or false): specifies whether the video is played automatically (true by default).

- **LOOP** (true or false): indicates whether the video is played in a loop (false by default).

Example

```
<EMBED SRC="my_film.mpg" HEIGHT="240"
    WIDTH="320"AUTOSTART="true"LOOP="true">
    </EMBED>
```

Particular features of RealVideo

Metafile

The source file of a sequence in Real format has the extension .rpm. It merely designates the URL of the video file in .rm format. So the **SRC** attribute must point to this source file, known as a *metafile*. A simple text editor suffices to create the metafile – remember to save it with the extension .rpm.

Here's an example of the entire contents of a metafile:

http://www.my_site.domain/video/my_clip.rpm

Setting the EMBED tag

The syntax of control attributes differs somewhat from other formats. The controls are shown using the attribute **CONTROLS**, which can take many values – in particular:

- ▶ **All**: all the controls are shown in the console.

- ▶ **ImageWindow**: The console is reserved for showing the video clip. The controls are accessible via the contextual menu (right-click in the window).

- ▶ **PlayButton**: Only the buttons **Play** and **Pause** are shown.

- ▶ **StopButton**: Only the **Stop** button is shown.

Each control element forms an independent entity. **ImageWindow** will apply at the very least. Each new controller is displayed by specifying a new **EMBED** tag. The various controllers are linked using the attribute **CONSOLE**, the value of which must be the same for each controller.

Example

```
<EMBED SRC="my_film.rpm" HEIGHT="240"
    WIDTH="320" AUTOSTART="true"
```

```
        CONTROLS="ImageWindow"
        CONSOLE="my_film"></EMBED>
```

Then the console of the controller "Play":

```
<P><EMBED SRC="my_film.rpm" HEIGHT="24"
        WIDTH="40"CONTROLS="PlayButton"
        CONSOLE="my_film"></EMBED></P>
```

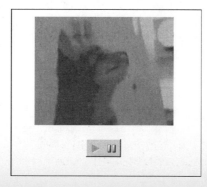

5.5. Webcams

Webcams are the electronic eyes of the Web. They have been proliferating for some years now, invading every nook and cranny of the planet. The prime purpose of these minicameras, videoconferencing, is a science fiction dream now come true. With a specialised software application (such as Microsoft NetMeeting), anyone can now converse live and using video with associates, col-

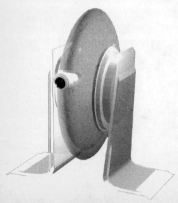

leagues and friends throughout the world. Today, Webcams are featured on Web sites as well, often in personal pages, where many Net surfers lay bare their privacy by placing these little spies in their bedroom, their drawing room, even… in their fridge!! Tourism Web sites dedicated to Webcams spy on famous monuments and places (see *www.earthcam.com*). The show is free most of the time, often accompanied by sound. The image quality varies widely depending on the performance of the camera. In any event, the image provided by a Webcam is inferior to that of a standard camera. It is always highly compressed, and its resolution rarely exceeds 320 x 200 pixels.

These cameras, which can now be had for something like £30, are connected through a parallel port, a USB port (where the bytestream is faster) or, though more rarely, through a video acquisition card.

Unlike the case with other videos, the shots are not inserted into a Web page as a sequence, but as an image (JPEG) refreshed at regular intervals. A "session" is therefore conducted online, in real time, and requires constant communication with the server, to which the images are transmitted and then updated on the Web site. An *FTP* module is therefore indispensable. Many software applications, often supplied with the camera, are specialised for this function (for instance, ISpy and Webcam32). They display the FTP address of the server on which the Web page is hosted, the name and location of the page, and the refresh interval. This interval must not be too short, to give the image time to be transferred. But in most cases you'll not want it to be too long, either... A good average is 30 seconds to a minute (maximum).

New York city as if you were there...

In terms of HTML code, the image is inserted just like any other by means of the tag **<IMG>**, with its size specified. In the page header, a refresh specification will cause the contents of the page to be updated regularly. At the specified intervals, the page will be refreshed and the image overwritten by the new Webcam shot, for the entire length of the session.

Example

```
<HEAD>
<META http-equiv="refresh" content="30">
</HEAD>


<BODY>
<IMG SRC="Webcam.jpg" width="320" height="200">
<BODY>
```

Note

A Java applet can carry out the same functions as these applications.

6. Animated GIFs

6.1. Introduction

Animated GIFs were the first moving images to appear on the Web. Initially employed on animated advertising banners, menus and buttons, this format proved to be a simple and effective means of drawing attention and giving Web pages that spark of life they had often lacked. These ancestors of more recent animation techniques have been around for a long time and indeed are still used.

GIF (Graphic Interchange Format, developed by CompuServe) is a highly compressed graphic format that retains quite a good image quality, and so is ideally suited for the Internet. GIF compression can be applied only to images with a maximum palette of 256 (8-bit) colours, and results in areas of solid colour. For these reasons, photographs and graphics with many shades of colours suffer under GIF compression. In such cases, JPEG (Joint Photographic Experts Group), the other major standard for the Internet, is used. GIF, however, is ideal for logos, texts and suchlike graphics.

When it appeared in 1989, GIF89a ushered in the age of animated images on the Web. This format can be used to save a series of images in a single file with the extension .gif. It also contains control information about the sequence (duration, loop count, etc.).

This is naturally reflected in the size of the file, and animated GIFs most often consist of only two images, or more rarely about half a dozen, and are never real animated clips.

An animated GIF is created in two steps, which usually require two different software applications.

▶ The first step can be handled by any graphic application that can save images in .gif format, which will be used to create the static component images. There are many such applications, their price depending on the number and complexity of their functions. We should mention in particular Adobe Photoshop and Paint Shop Pro for creating bitmap images, and Adobe Illustrator and Macromedia FreeHand for vector images.

▶ The second step requires an image animation application that can handle the .gif format. Once again, there are many such applications, including:

- GIF Construction Set Professional, Alchemy Mindworks:

  www.mindworkshop.com/alchemy/gifcon.html

- GIF Movie Gear, Gamani Productions, 30-day trial version:

  www.gamani.com/gmgdown.htm

- Ulead GIF Animator 4.0, Ulead Systems, 15-day trial version:

www.ulead.com/ga/trial.htm

Note

Some specifically Web-oriented tools such as Adobe ImageReady and Macromedia Fireworks can be used for both steps.

6.2. Creating a GIF animation with GIF Movie Gear

After you've installed the executable file (just over a megabyte to download), run the program. A dialogue box opens, featuring three tabs.

▶ The first (*Show Tutorial*) gives access to a comprehensive tutorial in **.htm** format. If you take the time to run it, you will learn much more than from this quick introduction…

▶ The second, *Open Existing Animation*, enables you to import an existing animation or image to be processed. The formats supported by GIF Movie Gear are .gif, .avi, .ani (animated cursors), .gif, .jpeg, .bmp (the Windows graphic format) and .psd (the Photoshop format). Note that this operation can be carried out subsequently (with **File/Import From…**).

The imported sequence will be broken down into frames that you can then manipulate as explained below. You can use **Frames/Reduce** to delete frames at a frequency of 1 to X.

▶ Click the **Start from Scratch** tab to launch the program proper.

To begin, open the frames that you created earlier using a graphic application. Select **File/Insert Frame(s)…** You can insert the frames one by one, in the order you wish (but remember that a frame is always inserted before the one opened previously). Hold down the **Ctrl** key, select all the constituent frames of your animation, and click **OK**.

You now have your sequence, broken down as indicated in this illustration.

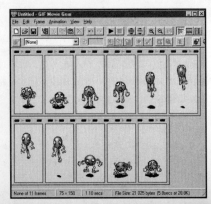

The **View/Animation Preview** command provides a preview of the result, and you should not hesitate to use it as you work.

You can arrange the frames with simple drag/drop operations, and you can use **Frames/Reverse Order** to reverse the order of the images if the animation is to be played in reverse.

You can use numerous functions on the entire animation or on each frame to:

- Modify the size of the images (**Frame/Move Crop** or **Animation/Crop** and **Resize** commands);

- Change the colour palette (**Animation/Reduce Colors**) in order to optimise the size of the final file;

- Specify the duration of the various frames (globally with **Frames/Global Properties**; individually with **Frames/Properties**). The default duration is 1/10th of a second;

- Define the number of times the sequence is repeated (**Animation/Properties**). The animation is played in a loop by default (zero value).

Once you have entered these different settings, save your work. The .gif format will be proposed by default. However, you can use the **File/Export As** command to create an .avi file or an animated cursor.

Note: Transparency

As we've already pointed out, one advantage of the GIF format is that it can manage transparency. Consequently, an image need no longer be set in a rectangular frame, and can adjust to any background colour.

To create a transparent background, select **Frames/Global Properties**. The central field contains two checkmark boxes. The first, **Interlace**, affects the way the image is displayed on the screen. An interlaced image will appear gradually, with increasing quality (which reduces the perceived waiting time). Once ticked, the second box, **Transparent**, gives access to a new window. You can use the eyedropper to choose the colour or colours that are to be transparent. Repeat the entries to attenuate the milling effect on the outline borders of the image. Make sure you don't choose a colour already present elsewhere in the image, because you'll then get "holes". This is where preliminary creative work can be useful.

7. Vector animation: Flash

Since it first appeared on the Web design scene in 1997, Flash has been much in vogue. By combining several powerful technologies, this software application has revolutionised animation on the Web. Ushering in a new standard based on vector images and on continuous streaming, Flash has managed to overcome transfer-rate and compatibility problems that considerably limited multimedia downloading.

Powerful interactive and animation functions, along with ease of use and the virtually unlimited creativity it allows, make this application an essential tool in Web site design.

Flash 5 is available in a 30-day demo version on countless CD-ROMs included with computer magazines, or you can download it directly from the Macromedia Flash site (*www.macromedia.com/software/flash*).

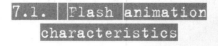

7.1. Flash animation characteristics

Vector image

There are two rival technologies in the digital image world: bitmap image and vector image.

▸ A bitmap image is composed of pixels, the number of which depend on its resolution. Each pixel contains luminosity and colour data. The image is formed by juxtaposing such data. The larger the image, the more pixels it will have, and the larger the size of the graphic file. The most widespread bitmap formats on the Web are GIF and JPEG.

▸ A vector image is created by mathematical operations that define vectors. These determine the size, shape, colour and position of an element – so resolution is of no importance here. Unlike the case with a bitmap image, the size of a vector image does not affect the size of the file. Vector images, which are particularly suitable for typography, cartoons, buttons etc., are far smaller in size than are their bitmap counterparts.

The same image in bitmap and vector versions.

Streaming

Shockwave Flash (.swf) is a streaming format for continuous playing. Used with small-sized files, it considerably reduces the time taken to download animations.

Compatibility

Animating objects using script languages often poses restrictive compatibility problems. Flash gets around this by supplying its own external plug-in (although, unlike Java, for example, Flash is still not well established under Linux and BeOS).

The Flash plug-in (Shockwave Flash Player) is integrated into the latest versions of browsers or can be downloaded free of charge from *www.macromedia.com/shockwave*. According to Macromedia, 92% of all surfers already have it on their systems.

7.2. | Main Flash functions: a brief outline

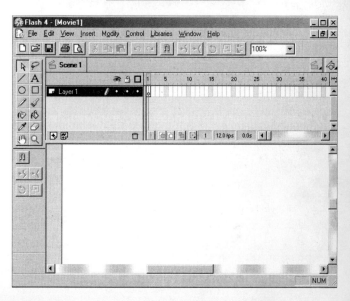

The tool palette

 The Flash tool bar includes drawing tools for creating vector shapes: texts, lines, Bezier curves, polygons etc. The editing tools in the lower part come in very handy for adjusting freehand drawings. Flash has shape-recognition functions that can be used to refine or straighten out curves, segments or joined lines. The Arrow tool can be used to move or edit a shape by adjusting its control points.

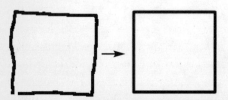

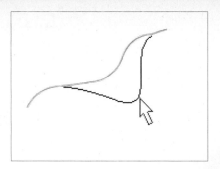

Editing a Bezier curve with the Arrow tool.

Symbols

Each image created in Flash can become a symbol. Stored in the *Library*, symbols are objects that can be used several times in an animation without affecting the size of the final file, because the symbol is stored in memory only once. Each occurrence can also be edited in place (colour, text, actions, etc.).

There are three types of symbols:

▸ Graphics – These are static elements (decors, backgrounds,
etc.) that can be used several
times in an animation.

▸ Buttons – Thanks to a specific *scenario* (see below),
Flash manages the interactive use of buttons very easily and effectively with the mouse. There are three
types of button, corresponding to the following states:
normal, onMouseOver and onClick. The sensitive
area of the button is
defined by a fourth
shape.

▸ Animation clips – These clips are short, independent
animations that can be imported into the main *scene*

(see below). They have their own scenario and can contain their own sounds, buttons and interactive functions.

The scene and the scenarios

The *scene* is the main window in which the animation is played. A Flash animation can be composed of several scenes played in succession or in response to an action.

The various constituent elements, symbols and other objects of the animation are placed in the scene. The behaviour of each of these elements is managed in an independent window, known as the *scenario*, indicating the moment at which an element is to appear, the length of time it is to be displayed and any actions it is to perform (interactive functions, sound event, etc.).

Animation

An animation can be created in Flash in two different ways: image animation by image, or interpolated.

▸ *Image animation by image* is the traditional method used in cartoons. It is also the more tedious. Images are created one after the other, each slightly different from the previous one, corresponding to different stages of a movement. Arranged in a time line (the scenario), they are 'read' in sequence by the reading head and displayed as motion.

An image animation by image is larger in size than an interpolated image, as each of its constituent images must be saved independently in the final file.

▸ An *interpolated animation* is created by the computer, which calculates intermediate stages between two key images. With this method, it is possible to create not only rotations, translations, etc., but also distortions. This latter technique, known as *morphing*, is used to transform one shape into another, or to change the colour, size or transparency of an object. Depending on the particular situation, creating an interpolated image can be a rather complicated process, and requires a certain level of experience.

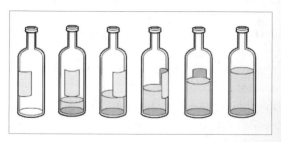

Layers

Just as in the most sophisticated graphic software applications, Flash too features layers. Extremely varied and powerful for creative purposes, layers are used in particular to position and animate objects on independent planes.

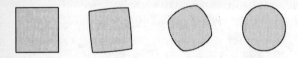

Interactivity

Flash owes its success largely to its powerful interactive functions. These are so advanced that many games developed with Flash are now on the Web.

As in JavaScript, the interaction is managed by *events*. These are associated with the mouse, the keyboard or the reading of an image and launch of an action. The **Actions** tab in the **Image properties** dialogue box features some 20 actions such as animation control, call a link or open a new animation. These actions can be interlinked or run in sequence, thereby increasing the interactive potential of Flash. Finally, the application has its own script language in which you can program actions. The grammar of this relatively simple language uses operators, variables and functions. So if you handled the chapter on JavaScript without getting discouraged, you won't have much difficulty programming your own Flash functions.

The various media

Designed to create multimedia and interactive content for the Web, Flash is used to integrate fixed or animated videos, sounds and video sequences in the same animation. It supports the standard Internet formats.

Sound

Adding sound to Web pages gives them an added dimension that can create a particular ambience and make interactive functions more concrete. And these are precisely the objectives of the sound functions integrated into this software application.

Flash supports the two standard Windows and Macintosh sound formats, .wav and AIFF files. Once imported, a sound can be associated with an event or played continuously (as a background sound or as an audio track synchronised with an animation). The **Sound** tab in the **Image properties** dialogue box is used to edit and change sounds. The edit window includes the digital representation of the two channels of a stereo sound, which have their own scenario. You can tinker with the various controls to sample a sound clip, adjust the volume in different places, set the controls, etc.

Finally, Flash has its own sound file compression and optimisation tools to export sounds as MP3. Oddly enough, this application cannot import sounds coded under this format.

Bitmaps

A vector image does not make for a high degree of realism. For instance, you may wish to use a photo or a much more natural image in an animation. Well, you can. The bitmap import function supports many formats (such as .bmp or Pict, PNG, JPEG and GIF). Once imported, bitmap images can be optimised and even converted into vector images by means of a plotting function.

Bitmap image.

Vector image.

Video

Thanks to the QuickTime capacities of Flash, Flash animations can be combined with video sequences in QuickTime format – to create interactive videos, for instance.

Publishing an animation

Although it is possible to create a Web page entirely in Flash, a .swf animation is usually inserted into the HTML document.

Flash boasts very complete publication functions. For the sake of simplicity, we can say that there are three different publication methods:

1 **Flash animation embedded in an HTML page**

   The animation, in .swf format, is inserted into a blank HTML page by means of the tags **<EMBED>** and **<OBJECT>** (see Chapter 4.1).

This function can also detect whether the surfer who will view the page has the Flash player, and it can display a replacement image (in GIF, JPEG or PNG format) if that is not the case.

You can also simply save the animation in .swf format and import it into an HTML page by means of a Web page editor that supports Flash, such as Dreamweaver (developed by Macromedia, and thus optimally compatible).

2 Flash projection

A *projection* is an executable file that contains the Flash animation and the components required to read it; so you don't need the Flash plug-in to view it. You simply download the .exe file and then run it, and the animation is played in an independent window. Note that this solution is well suited to off-line projection.

3 QuickTime animation

Cooperation between Macromedia and Apple has made it possible to publish Flash animations in .mov format, which can be played by all users who have the QuickTime plug-in.

If a QuickTime sequence has been combined with a Flash animation, this solution is the only alternative.

Note: Macromedia Director

Indispensable for multimedia production, this software application is probably the most complete and efficient interactive multimedia content creation tool on the market today. Although it can be used to create touch-screen kiosks, this package is also perfectly suitable for the Web, for creating Shockwave animations that are streamed and automatically integrated into HTML pages.

Director is a powerful multimedia content-creation tool. It can combine text, sounds (Shockwave Audio, MP3, AIFF, .wav etc.), bitmap or vector images (for which it has its own creation tools), digital animations (.avi, QuickTime and QuickTime VR) or Flash animations in the same sequence.

Thanks to *behaviours* and its proprietary script language (Lingo), Director can also be used to create interactive functions such as rollovers, animation controls, sound synchronisation, reactions to mouse clicks, link calls etc.

Director animations (.dcr) require Shockwave Player 8 or later (download from *www.macromedia.com/shockwave*).

Note: Adobe LiveMotion

Adobe has also launched into the world of animation for the Web with Adobe LiveMotion, which is expected to rival Flash. Fortunately, the company has opted for established Web standards, so that LiveMotion (.liv) animations can be exported to Flash and GIF formats. New features of this program worth particular mention include a global approach based on the ergonomics and functions of Photoshop – with a similar way of dealing with layers, filters, drop-shadow effects, textures etc. Nor is interaction wanting, but the vector shape-creation tools are not up to the flexibility and complexity of the equivalent Flash functions.

8. 3D and virtual reality on the Internet

Although virtual reality has been the rage on game consoles and cinema screens for a number of years, it is still rather limited and discreet on the Internet. Nevertheless, everybody knows that there are 'virtual worlds' – all those chat rooms where surfers can assume the characters they want and interact with the setting and the other characters present. These multi-user 'cyberworlds' are becoming increasingly more sophisticated, to the point of being parallel worlds in which you can build your own house, earn virtual money and so forth.

But there are other 3D applications on the Web. For instance, objects can be presented from every side and handled easily with the mouse – an undeniable advantage for commercial sites and galleries in particular, for these technologies open up interesting, unprecedented prospects for browsing.

Today, virtual reality on the Web is still a long way from vying with off-line image technologies such as television or the cinema, because, once again, these technologies require the transfer of a large amount of data.

In general, to view objects in three dimensions or to visit these virtual worlds, surfers have to install specific plug-ins on their browsers, although these are free of charge.

There are three major technologies in 3D and virtual reality, although there are many other developments and things on this front are constantly changing.

8.1. Virtual Reality Modelling Language (VRML)

The first virtual worlds, which caused such a stir when they first arrived on the Net, owed their existence to VRML. Created in 1994, this language gradually conquered the Web, in spite of its relatively obscure existence. However, its second version opened up new dynamic prospects such as interactions and a sound environment, and now VRML seems to be winning new users.

Although VRML documents are simple ASCII files, creating them means having to learn the language, which is rather complex, although related to HTML. The various objects are created first in skeletal form, then textured and smoothed out, and finally put in a definitive mould. The various elements are then assembled in an environment to create a virtual world. Having brought about a change of appearance, surfers can use the keyboard or mouse to travel in a setting where the views are refashioned with every movement. They may encounter obstacles and interact with them (these may stop surfers or constitute a link to another setting) or with other users. In this way, these virtual worlds are gigantic discussion forums and, although the conversations are conducted in text mode, the graphical universe gives them an ambience all their own.

8.2.   3D Markup Language (3DML)

Unlike VRML, using 3DML requires no modelling, but resembles a building-block game such as Lego, where various predefined objects are assembled into complex configurations called *spots*. Cubes, columns, walls, trees etc. are all basic elements drawn from a massive library, which are arranged and modified to create a house, a street, a ground, a landscape and so on. All that is needed then is to define the ground, sky, light and texture parameters, and a virtual world is born! (This is rather simplifying the process, but the underlying principle is there.) The surfer advances in it by relying on the mouse for guidance, in a manner very similar to travelling in a VRML world.

8.3.   QuickTime Virtual Reality

In QuickTime VR from Apple, an object or a space can be manipulated in all three dimensions. Online and on

CD-ROM, numerous virtual-visit systems (famous sites, museums, virtual galleries and auction sites, among others) avail themselves of this technology. Unlike VRML and 3DML, QuickTime VR is not a language, but a technology featuring real objects as films in .mov format managed by QuickTime Player 4.

The Louvre museum.

A QuickTime VR document is formed by a computer-ised concourse of multiple rotating shots of the same space (or object).

QuickTime VR offers many advantages (realism, sounds, texts, zoom etc.), but the size of its files is a serious handicap for use on the Net (on the other hand, this technology is very suited to interactive CD-ROMs).

8.4 | Integrating 3D objects into a Web page

As in all media, you can opt for a dynamic solution (a hypertext link to a file with the proper extension), or for integration into the page itself with the tags **<EMBED>** or **<OBJECT>**. In the latter case, you must also define the size of the object or scene.

Examples

▶ Hypertext link:

`<A HREF="file_name.wrl">Click here</A>`

▶ File embedded with the tag **`<EMBED>`**:

`<EMBED SRC="file_name.wrl" WIDTH=800 HEIGHT=400></EMBED>`

8.5. Plug-ins

VRML and 3DML files require a plug-in for your browser. There are several such plug-ins, for specific browsers:

▶ **VRML (.wrl)**

Cosmo Player (Internet Explorer 4.0 and Netscape Communicator 4.0, or later):
www.cai.com/cosmo/home.htm

For information on VRML browsers, go to:

www.Web3d.org/VRML/browpi.htm

▸ **3DML (.3dml)**

Flatland Rover 2.0 for Microsoft (beta version for Macintosh):

www.flatland.com/download/

▸ **QuickTime VR (.mov)**

QuickTime Player 4 (Mac and PC):

www.apple.com/quicktime/download

Appendices

A. Words reserved by JavaScript

The following words cannot be used when creating an object, variable or function:

abstract	boolean	break	byte	case	catch
char	class	const	continue	debugger	default
delete	do	double	else	enum	export
extends	false	final	finally	float	for
function	goto	if	implements	import	in
instanceof	int	interface	long	native	new
null	package	private	protected	public	return
short	static	super	switch	synchronised	this
throw	throws	transient	true	try	typeof
var	void	volatile	while	with	

B. Hierarchy of main JavaScript objects

The main JavaScript objects are listed below according to their hierarchy. Each is followed by a brief description and some of the object's properties.

▶ **window**
The browser window: innerHeight, innerWidth, location, status, etc.

■ **document**
The HTML page: bgColor, forms, images, links, etc.

■ **area**
Image map: href, target, etc.

■ **images**
Image: border, name, height, width, src, lowsrc, etc.

- **links**

Link call: href, target, etc.

- **forms**

Form: name, elements, etc.

- **button**

Button in a form: name, value, etc.

- **checkbox**

Checkbox in a form: name, value, etc.

- **password**

Password in a form: name, value, etc.

- **radio**

Radio-button in a form: name, value, etc.

- **reset**

Reset-button in a form: name, value, etc.

- **select**

Selection-list in a form: name, value, etc.

- **submit**

Submit-button in a form: name, value, etc.

- **text**

Line of text in a form: name, value, etc.

- **textarea**

Area of text in a form: name, value, etc.

- **frames**

Set of elements of a frameset. The following keywords are used to indicate the specific frame addressed:

self (current frame), parent (higher-level frame) and top (highest-level frame).

Example:
```
---------
Parent.frames().document.images2.src="image3.jpg"
```

- **location**

Current URL: href, etc.

- **history**

URL used.

- **navigator**

Browser used: appName, appVersion, language, etc.

C. Useful addresses

Good global resources

- *http://www.web-authoring.com*
- *http://www.webmasters-resources.com*
- *http://www.wdvl.com*
- *http://www.webmonkey.com*
- *http://www.webreference.com*
- *http://www.webdeveloper.com*

Scripts to download

- *http://www.scriptsearch.com*

JavaScript

- *http://www.javascript.com*

DHTML

- *http://www.dhtmlzone.com*

Java applets

- *http://javaboutique.internet.com*

Flash

- *http://www.flashplanet.com*
- *http://www.flashkit.com*

D. Glossary

3DML (3D Markup Language)

Language for describing virtual worlds ("spots"), similar to HTML. It was developed by the Flatland company.

ActiveX

Set of technologies to link and incorporate objects between applications, developed by Microsoft as a competitor to Java. ActiveX controls (which can be written in several languages) are mainly used to manage the insertion of objects into Web pages. ActiveX controls also permit the development of applets.

Animated GIF

An animated GIF is a file in the GIF 89a format that combines several images that display one after another and thus create an animated sequence. Special software is required to create an animated GIF.

Applet

Tiny application – most often written in Java and compiled – that combines with a Web page to add features to it. When written in Java, an applet can be run on all platforms.

Argument (JavaScript)

The "arguments" of a JavaScript function are the set of externally-supplied variables necessary to run it.

Attribute (HTML)

Parameter of an HTML item.

AVI

AVI is the video format standard for Windows. AVI files are of high quality but are fairly large and thus are inconvenient for use on the Web.

Browser

Software designed for navigating the Net. It is within a browser that Web pages are displayed. The two most common browsers are Internet Explorer from Microsoft and Netscape Communicator from Netscape.

CGI (Common Gateway Interface)

Software data communication interface between a Web server and other programs running on remote computers. CGI scripts are mainly used to process data entered into forms.

Condition

JavaScript conditional instructions make the execution of a function dependent on a binary test (logical operator of the form if... then...) or a multiple test (comparison with several possible values).

Cookie

Information stored in a file on the Internet user's computer when he or she visits a site. This data is read and used when the site is revisited to identify the user and recall his or her preferences.

CSS (Cascading Style Sheets)

Style sheets are an important feature of HTML 4.0. They allow the definition of a layout style for all items of a Web page and also allow the developer to control the exact positioning of items on the page (CSS-Positioning or CSS-P).

DHTML (Dynamic HTML)

Dynamic HTML is the technology used to animate Web pages and extend their interactive functions. DHTML brings together HTML 4, JavaScript and some style-sheet properties.

DOM (Domain Object Model)

The Domain Object Model is a syntax that allows script languages to access an HTML object to edit its properties. Even though this syntax is supposed to be a standard, it varies from browser to browser (Netscape or Microsoft Explorer).

Download

To get data (software, images, text, etc.) from a distant computer via the Internet.

Event (JavaScript)

JavaScript events allow the triggering of a function at a pre-specified instant, such as following a user action, on loading a Web page, etc. The processing of events makes the running of scripts non-linear and provides powerful interactivity.

Flash

Name of Macromedia's software for handling vector images. This program, equipped with powerful interactive functions, allows the creation of graphics and animations for a Web site. These are very small in size but require the installation of a plug-in (available for free) so that they can be displayed by the browser.

FTP (File Transfer Protocol)

Protocol for transferring files via the Internet. FTP allows downloading of files from or uploading of files to a remote computer. Setting up a Web site requires the use of an FTP client (software program) to transfer the files of the site to the Web server.

Function (JavaScript)

Action or actions on one or more JavaScript objects whose execution leads to a result that itself depends on variables.

Predefined functions available in the JavaScript syntax are called "methods".

GIF (Graphic Interchange Format)

Bitmap graphic format that is very common on the Web because of its compressibility. This "non-lossy" compression works only on images with up to 256 colours and is particularly suited to images using flat colours.

GIF89a

Derivative of the GIF format that appeared in 1989 and which, compared to the previous version (87), incorporates new features such as interlacing and animation (see "Animated GIF").

HTML (Hyper Text Markup Language)

Language used to describe Web pages. It is used to create documents (sites) published on the Internet.

Hypertext

The basic principle behind the interactivity of Web pages. This technique allows the interconnection of different Web pages using "links". A mouse click on a link (text or image) invokes a URL and a new page is loaded into the browser. Hypertext enables a new, non-linear mode for accessing information.

Internet

The world-wide communication network that connects hundreds of millions of users. The Internet consists of several services each governed by its own protocol for exchanging data. The service that is the most used is, of course, the Web, but other services include newsgroups, e-mail, FTP, etc.

Java

Object-oriented programming language developed by Sun Microsystems. A program (applet or other) written in Java can be executed on any platform that integrates a "virtual Java machine" which interprets and executes Java instructions.

JavaScript

Programming language originally created by Netscape. JavaScript, very different from Java, allows the writing of small applications (scripts) that can be included in Web pages and which are interpreted along with the HTML code. In principle, the script is run by the browser on the client computer.

JPEG (Joint Photographic Experts Group)

JPEG is one of the most used bitmap graphics standards on the Internet. It is especially suited to photographic images. The higher the JPEG compression used, the greater is the loss of quality of the image.

JScript

This is the version of JavaScript that Microsoft has implemented in Internet Explorer.

MPEG (Moving Picture Expert Group)

Set of video compression formats. Mpeg-2 is used to compress video data on DVD.

Multimedia

Collection of different media (text, images, sound, video, etc.) grouped together on the same computer medium (CD-ROM, Web page, etc.).

Object (JavaScript)

Set of data that is predefined or defined by the user that can be edited using JavaScript functions.

Off-line

In our context, off-line means the usage of Internet services in "local" mode, i.e., when the computer is not connected to the Internet.

Online

Usage of Internet services when the connection is active.

Plug-in

Software program that attaches to another to increase the features of the latter. When integrated into the browser, several plug-ins allow it to recognise file formats that are not supported by default (Flash, for example).

QuickTime

Video format standard from Apple. QuickTime files are of high quality but are large. Versions 3 and later incorporate streaming.

QuickTime VR

Video technology developed by Apple to create three-dimensional scenes within which one can move using the mouse. A plug-in is required to view such files.

RealMedia

This term designates two coding formats for sound files (RealAudio) and video files (RealVideo) that were developed by the RealNetworks company. Their main feature is that of streaming.

Rollover

Interactive technique incorporated in HTML that allows the alternation of one image with another when a mouse moves over it.

Script

A script is a small application whose source-code is to be embbeded in a Web page. The syntax of script languages is very simple compared to other, more developed, languages (Java, C++,...), which makes them accessible to a larger group of programmers.

Server

A remote computer connected to the Internet that provides different services to Internet users (display of Web pages, hosting, e-mail, etc. ...).

Shockwave

Format used by Macromedia Director software that allows the creation of interactive multimedia content that can be incorporated within Web pages and distributed as continuous flow. Shockwave is also the name of the plug-in necessary to view such files.

Streaming

Continuous-flow data-distribution technology for sound and video. The playing starts as the file begins to download. If there are interruptions in the flow, a certain quantity of information that is kept in buffer memory is used to continue the playback.

Tag

Tags are the same as HTML commands. They often use several parameters (attributes).

URL (Uniform Resource Locator)

System of allocating Internet addresses. More generally, the URL designates the address of a Web site.

Variable

Data type that can take different values.

VBScript

Script language developed by Microsoft. As with JavaScript, it is intended for creating small applications for Web pages. However, because of incompatibilities with Netscape Communicator, VBScript is less commonly used.

VRML (Virtual Reality Modelling Language)

Language for modelling virtual worlds. Installation of a plug-in is necessary to view a VRML scene.

Web or WWW

Abbreviation of World Wide Web. The Web is the multimedia part of the Internet.

Webcam

Miniature camera capable of taking snapshots (of rather low resolution) at regular intervals and of sending them to the Internet (as part of a videoconference or for display on a Web page).

Wizard

Software process that guides the user during the execution of a given task.

WYSIWYG (What You See Is What You Get)

Said of any software that displays a document on the screen exactly as it will be seen or printed. WYSIWYG HTML editors allow the creation of Web pages without the user having to deal with the underlying HTML code.

Zip

Standard compression format which allows significant reduction in the size of a file. The file has to be uncompressed before use.

Index